The Sweet Shack and Bach Bar

Heather MacKenzie-Carey

This book is a work of fiction. Names, characters, places, and incidents are the product of the author's imagination or are used fictitiously. Any resemblance to actual events, locales, or persons, living or dead, is coincidental.

Copyright 2011 Heather MacKenzie-Carey

All rights reserved. No part of this publication may be reproduceed or transmitted in any form or by any means, electronic or mechanical, including photocopying, recording, or any information storage and retrieval system, without permission in writing from the publisher.

Edited by Clare Marshall and Kathleen Healy
Cover design by Adam Murray

Printed and bound in Canada at Friesens

Cataloging information available at Library and Archives Canada

First printing 2011

10 9 8 7 6 5 4 3 2 1

Published in 2011 by Bryler Publications Inc.

Suite 1035,
Chester, NS
B0J 1J0
Visit our website at www.brylerpublications.com

This book is dedicated to Wise Woman everywhere;
past, present and future.
To all those who have been with me at various times in my
life, I thank you for helping shape me into who I am.
You have always, and continue to, balance me, push me,
pick me up, and encourage me.
Most of all, in true Wise Woman fashion, you listened.

Introduction

We have a strong connection to food. Just the smell of a favourite recipe can instantly link you to a past memory, or seal an experience in the present and make it memorable. For many cultures, it is during the preparation and serving of food that stories are told, secrets are shared, experiences are relived, and feelings are soothed.

The Wise Woman and Merlin exist in a dimension that you only discover when you need it. In each of the seven chapters, a different person stumbles into the Sweet Shack and Bach Bar and is served a dessert that helps with the problems they are struggling with. As they describe their situations, the Wise Woman provides shots of the Bach Flowers that will help balance their emotions. When they leave the bar, each character receives a symbol or magically acquired gift that helps them on their journey.

The Wise Woman understands that certain foods have a connection to the chakras or energy centres within our bodies. It is by no accident that we associate foods with the comfort we may have received from them in an earlier time.

All the recipes in this book are real and can be replicated. You can find them at the back of this book. The Wise Woman has carefully chosen each of the recipes to provide comfort for that chakra. It is important to note that the Wise Woman does not measure ingredients too carefully. If she measures at all, it is an approximation for the reader's benefit, but you should use your own taste and discretion to get the best results. She is not very exacting or scientific in her approach to cooking. The Wise Woman believes this is the way great discoveries are made, and she encourages you to do the same.

All Wise Women make great bartenders because they have perfected the art of listening. In the Bach Bar, shot glasses contain Bach Flower essences rather than alcohol. The Bach Flower essences are real and readily available in most health food stores, as well as through Internet sources. Many alternative healers and naturopathic physicians use Bach Flowers in their practices. This collection of thirty-eight healing essences was developed over one-hundred years ago by Dr. Edward Bach. He intended the essences to be a self-help method of healing. Dr. Bach believed all diseases occur because of an imbalance of emotions, and that by balancing your thoughts and emotions your body could naturally heal itself. As the Wise Woman listens to her guests' stories, she provides a shot glass of the Bach Flower essence that matches the predominant emotional imbalance they are describing. Her descriptions of the essences' healing effects are in line with Dr. Bach's intentions. In her footnotes at the end of each chapter, the Wise Woman ties the Bach Flower essences to the chakra imbalance the person is experiencing.

The shot glass presentation of the Bach Flower essences is unique to the Sweet Shack and Bach Bar experience. Bach Flowers are more commonly mixed as two to four drops of each essence in a small bottle of spring water. They are often taken in combination with other remedies rather than the individual shots that Wise Woman provides. You typically take four drops of this mixture, four times per day, for long term use or as required in sudden, emergency situations.

In the Sweet Shack and Bach Bar guests often respond quite quickly and dramatically to the Bach Flower shots. True Bach Flower remedy therapy is usually more subtle in its approach, and the results are often experienced over a longer period of time.

Merlin, the Wise Woman's faithful companion, physically resembles a cat, but he is much more than that. Merlin is, among other things, quite an expert at chakras and colour therapy. Merlin understands that the chakras of the body are sources of energy that can be measured at certain vibration rates. These vibrations correspond to light waves, and can thus be expressed in colours. Merlin matches the appropriate colour to the chakra the person is experiencing an issue with, and provides gifts for guests that come through the Sweet Shack and Bach Bar.

The Wise Woman is a compilation of a number of people that I have been fortunate to encounter at various ages and stages in my life. Some of these people are still with me; others have moved on. At times I was aware that I was in the presence of someone very wise, receiving information that would be invaluable to me. At other times I was totally unaware, and later recognized the importance of that person in my life. For all of them, I am grateful. If during the reading of this book something strikes a chord for you, examine it. Try the Bach Flower essences if they seem to match for you. But above all, sit back, imagine yourself in the presence of a Wise Woman, and enjoy.

Heather MacKenzie-Carey

Chapter One

Samantha tried to steady her racing heart while her feet remained frozen in place. She had been in a hurry even before she saw the impending storm building in the distance. She had spent too much time fretting in front of the mirror about the suit she had picked up at the thrift store. She imagined how the suit's original owner felt three years ago when the suit was fashionable. That owner had probably picked it up on a whim, as it caught her eye in an expensive clothing store window on her way back from a luncheon with some powerful business executives. No doubt she took the purchase to her corner office with the million-dollar view of the city. At least, that was the dream Samantha had created when she saw the suit buried under a pile of cast-offs in the bin. She had further developed that character while she revitalized the suit by removing the stains and ironing out the creases.

No matter what she did to it, the next morning, the suit still looked like a reject. Who was she kidding, anyway? Did she think she could dress herself up to pretend to be more than what she was so that all of her dreams could come true? That was the stuff of fairy tales, like the ones that she read to her daughter Chloe every night. If anything, Samantha felt more like the Paper Bag Princess.

Twisting and turning in front of the mirror, she had felt

ridiculous in the ill-fitting suit with the worn, non-slip, ugly brown shoes she wore every day at the restaurant. Nobody saw your shoes when you stood at the drive-thru saying "Good afternoon, may I take your order please?" all day long. She must have been daydreaming when she applied for the library job in the first place. Maybe she had dreamed the whole phone conversation where a pleasant young man requested that she appear for an interview.

Because she had spent so much time trying to dream up a new character for herself, Samantha had left the house ten minutes later than she meant to. At least the ugly shoes were comfortable, so she was able to walk fast to make up some of the time.

Her dreams of having cab fare were interrupted when she heard the first distant clap of thunder. Her heart raced but her feet refused to move. Not now, not today, not when so much was at stake. The familiar sense of terror rose deep within her as she felt the electricity in the air. She knew she couldn't carry on. She jumped at the second clap of thunder and she realized her back had brushed up against something solid.

Even as she saw the flashing neon "Open" sign, another part of her mind struggled to put it in context. She walked by this part of the city every day when she dropped Chloe off at school. She knew there was no bar or restaurant here. This was one of the most fearful parts of her walk—there was an empty parking lot where old needles, condoms and cigarette butts advertised the night time activities. It reminded her how close she was to living in the streets, and the thought alone terrified her.

Samantha struggled to find reality as she opened the heavy oak door and walked inside a building that she knew couldn't be there. She stood on the threshold for just a moment as her eyes adjusted to the dim light and her mind argued with her soul. She felt the deep security of the solid oak floor beneath her feet. The soft lighting and the red velvet that covered the well-worn bar stools reminded her of her grandmother's living room couch. The warmth of the crackling fireplace soothed her. The smell of ginger cookies baking and that faint odour of old wood and heavy, worn fabric pulled her body forward while her mind traveled back to her memories.

Behind the bar was a woman who looked a little like her grandmother, rest her soul, with those long grey braids, and her no-nonsense, efficient attitude that was reflected in the way she moved around behind the counter, wiping the spots off glasses with just one swipe and lining them up in a row. The faded purple plaid flannel shirt looked comfortable and practical, if somewhat out of character for a bartender that was at least eighty years old. She looked more like the picture of a "Wise Woman" that Samantha held in her mind, mixed with the memory of her long-gone grandmother. None of it made sense and yet, Samantha found herself placing her bag on the floor and sitting down at the bar.

As she sat, her bag flopped over and clunked against the wood paneling of the bar. The noise startled a black cat who had been sitting on the stool next to Samantha. He yelped, launched into the air, landed on the floor beside Samantha, and bolted from the room. Startled at the sudden movement, Samantha felt her heart pounding once again as she clutched her chest.

"You'll be needing the special today." The Wise Woman bartender ignored the usual greetings of "Hi", "Nasty weather", or "What brings you in today" that bartenders usually engaged in. She didn't seem affected by the startled actions of both the cat and Samantha but she murmered, "Never mind Merlin, he'll come back when he gets his wits about him."

Before Samantha could protest that she had no money for anything let alone bar food and drink, or explain that she didn't have the time to be doing this on the way to an interview that could change her life if only she could get through it, the Wise Woman placed a plate of still-warm-from-the-oven ginger cookies in front of her.

"This is on the house," the Wise Woman claimed. "We're trying out a new recipe."

For a moment, Samantha's mind argued with the fact that bars don't serve ginger cookies as a house special, but the comforting scent of the spices and the sight of melting chocolate chunks oozing from the mound of dough felt much more real than anything else.

With the first small bite, Samantha started to cry. With the second bite, she started to talk, and like all good bartenders, the Wise Woman listened.

Samantha was terrified. She had been afraid of thunder and lightning ever since her childhood and now the thunder was getting louder, stronger, and shaking the building. She was scared she wouldn't find the money to pay her rent on the small one-bedroom apartment she shared with her daughter. She was scared she would live in poverty her entire life. She was scared that Social Services would take her daughter away. Samantha wept as she admitted she was scared of being attacked in the vacant parking lot. She was sure that her daughter's father still wanted to hurt her, even though she had broken away from the abusive relationship years ago. The fear lingered. The nightmares continued.

Samantha found herself staring at the empty shot glass without really remembering that she drank anything. The effect of the shot felt nothing like other shots she'd had in the past. In fact, it tasted like water. Samantha felt the fear lifting from her shoulders. The thunder seemed to be moving away.

"That was a shot of Rock Rose," the Wise Woman said before she could ask. "It's a Bach flower essence to help balance that deeply hidden fear of life itself. If you take a shot of Rock Rose, you can find courage and presence of mind. It will help you be calm so you can make rational decisions and move yourself forward to find the great courage you possess."

Merlin returned from parts unknown and cautiously approached the stool beside Samantha. She coaxed him closer with a piece of ginger cookie. She considered the Wise Woman's explanation as she shared a ginger cookie with the cat. He allowed her to scratch behind his ears while she ate. What was in that cookie? It felt so familiar to her, and yet, so far away, from another time.

She could remember how safe and secure she felt sitting on that red velvet couch listening to her grandmother tell her stories of strong, independent pioneer women who created lives for themselves and their children out of seemingly insurmountable problems. Samantha remembered how her grandmother had talked about inner strength and finding everything you needed within yourself. She dreamed of being back in her grandmother's house. Samantha had run away from her parents when she was eight, a few years younger than Chloe was now. Samantha had never really explained the abuse that had gone on in her parents' house, and her grandmother had never asked. Grandmother

Franklin had just taken her in, hugged her, fed her delicious food, and listened. So like the Wise Woman. There really was quite a resemblance. For years, Samantha had been safe and secure with Grandmother Franklin and she had never gone back to her old life. Samantha often wondered how things would have turned out if her grandmother hadn't stood up to her parents and refused to let them take Samantha back. Instead, she had raised Samantha as her own.

Then, in Samantha's final year of high school, Grandmother Franklin had died. Samantha's world was shattered. She had married Josh in a desperate attempt to fill the loneliness. When Samantha found she was pregnant with Chloe she thought the ache of despair might have lifted, but Josh quickly squashed that dream with alcohol, abuse and gambling that had dropped them all to the lowest point ever. Samantha knew she had been right to leave Josh, but she still doubted that she could ever create a comfortable life for Chloe. She often sat awake at night with a hot water bottle over her aching back, agonizing over the fact that they lived in a run-down apartment where the hot water ran out long before you could fill the bathtub, the elevator was always on the fritz, and the neighbours' cooking smells assaulted you first thing in the morning, as soon as you stepped into the hallway. Samantha had lost any hope of owning a real house. She wished Chloe could bring friends home from school, have parties and sleepovers, and enjoy the things Samantha never had. Lately, just checking the mail slot and waiting for the bills she couldn't pay to come was enough to make her feel close to a nervous breakdown. Tears flowed down her face as Samantha felt an intense sense of loneliness. She knew she was close to the limit of her endurance.

A second shot glass appeared and this time Samantha

drank the mixture without questioning what it might be. She felt safe with the Wise Woman. In fact, she didn't think she would ever leave this bar.

The Wise Woman pointed to the empty Bach flower shot glass. "It's Sweet Chestnut. It can help you when you have lost all hope and are filled with a sense of sorrow and loneliness so intense that you feel almost destroyed by it. Sometimes these feelings emerge when you've been going through years of difficulty or suffering and moving bravely through the world without complaining. Sometimes you need Sweet Chestnut when you are grieving someone. Life just catches up with you sometimes. Even though things around you might not change, Sweet Chestnut can help you face the world with a sense of optimism and peace of mind. Then you might discover that you do have a deep sense of inner support that will get you through."

Merlin, satisfied with both the cookies and the ear scratching, had curled up in Samantha's lap. His rhythmic breathing and her patting was so soothing Samantha settled into a new daydream as she savoured the last remaining ginger cookie. For a moment, she stopped to wonder how the cookie could still be warm, and the chocolate still melting. She had been there for so long, pouring out her whole life story to this woman that was, but didn't feel like, a stranger.

Once again, she felt herself back on her grandmother's couch, safe and secure with a stack of library books. The books had not replaced, but rather fuelled, her dreams. Samantha thought about how wonderful it would be to work in the library and help others pursue their dreams. She imagined walking home from work in a crisp pinstriped pantsuit. The jacket would be cut to flatter her shape in the latest style. She imagined the dangling ruby earrings she would wear to accent her personal style. She would be carrying an armload of books in a soft leather oversized purse when she stopped to pick Chloe and a friend up at the private school. She would make the girls hot chocolates with real marshmallows and chocolate chips and they would disappear to play together in Chloe's enormous room before supper. Samantha would settle into the red chaise longue in their spacious living room to review the new books before she catalogued them and took them back to place on the library shelves. Samantha imagined the latte she would make from her cappuccino machine. She would sip it from an oversized, wide mouthed, white mug.

Samantha was so content in her daydream that when Merlin jumped out of her lap with no warning, she thought she had spilled the latte! He hopped onto the bar and artfully stretched his back and swished his tail around another shot glass.

The Wise Woman smiled at the startled look on Samantha's face and scratched Merlin behind his ear. "Looks like you'll need that shot of Clematis. Clematis is for people that live in a world of their own."

Samantha downed the shot and nodded. "I have been accused of being a daydreamer, that's for sure."

"Clematis helps you take an interest in the world around you so that you can bring your dreams into reality," the Wise Woman explained. "When balanced, Clematis people see their dreams as inspiration and they can fulfill their creative potential. They sometimes bring their dreams into creative works of art, design, fashion, or writing. Clematis can help you root your feet securely in the earth while you pursue your sense of purpose in the present. You might even find yourself less absent-minded."

"Geez, my interview!" Samantha gasped as she looked at her watch. Strange. It was as though time had gone backwards while she was talking to the Wise Woman. She would still have enough time to leisurely walk to the library.

"I can do this." Samantha picked up her bag with her resume and notepad securely inside. It felt heavier to her than it had before and she looked in to see a pair of beautiful red shoes. They were made of soft leather with a low but distinct heel. They looked new, and yet, when she put them on they were exactly her size, like they had been moulded to her feet.

"You left those the last time you were here," Wise Woman said. "I'm glad you finally came back for them."

Samantha looked down at her feet and rolled her ankle in circles to admire the shoes. They were fashionable; perfect with the outfit. She felt strong, secure, grounded, and confident. She walked a city block feeling beautiful, smart, and with a sense of belonging. She knew she would get the job and she couldn't wait to go home and celebrate with Chloe, who would be so excited. Chloe loved books as much as her mother and her grandmother did. Maybe Samantha would splurge with the grocery money and buy something nice for supper to celebrate. That's when Samantha remembered she hadn't paid her bill. She turned back to the bar, wondering how she would explain that she didn't quite have the money yet.

The Sweet Shack and Bach Bar was gone. In its place was the empty parking lot, but somehow it didn't look the same. It didn't seem like a scary spot anymore.

A red breasted robin sat in the parking lot and Samantha could have sworn she heard the robin tell her to hurry up or she'd be late. She smiled, clicked the heels of her red shoes together in salute and strode away.

A Note from the Wise Woman

Samantha came to Merlin and I with issues of the first, or root chakra. The first chakra, lying in the region of the tailbone, is the lowest chakra and therefore sets the foundation for all the others. It is focused on stability, basic physical needs, self-preservation, trust, security and a sense of being grounded.

This chakra usually develops between one and eight years of age. At this time, a child develops the knowledge that his or her physical needs will be met. Towards the later phase of this development, children develop the ability to stand up for themselves. Major traumas such as divorce, physical injuries or death of a caregiver can upset the balanced development of this chakra. Events that threaten survival or even difficulty fitting in during the first years of school can cause problems later in life. For Samantha, physical abuse during this stage and separation from her parents might have contributed to later feelings of insecurity. Emotional problems linked to this chakra include bullying, self-centeredness, and an overly materialistic outlook. Increased risk-taking behaviour can also be a sign the root chakra is spinning too fast, or is considered to be too open. A blocked or sluggish first chakra can result in low self-esteem, emotionally needy or self-destructive behaviour. In Samantha's case, her blocked root chakra is expressed as extreme fear. Because of the foundational nature of this chakra, a person with problems in this area may experience back problems or bone disease. A person with a balanced root chakra tends to demonstrate self-mastery. They are physically healthy, well grounded, and full of energy.

Merlin and I made ginger cookies in anticipation of Samantha's arrival because ginger and cloves are spices that resonate with the root chakra. Cedar, rosemary, lime blossom and elderberry also resonate with this chakra and can be used for aromatherapy, but they don't make good cookies!

Emotional problems can often be addressed with the use of Bach Flower essences. The Bach flowers that may address problems of the root chakra include Rock Rose, Sweet Chestnut, and Clematis.

As I explained to Samantha, Rock Rose is used to subdue a real sense of terror, or "frozen with fear" behaviour. This is the fear that one's very survival is threatened. Rock Rose can be helpful for nightmares as well.

I gave Samantha Sweet Chestnut to help with her deep mental anguish. Sweet Chestnut is used when people feel they have reached the limit of their endurance and just can't carry on. It is often helpful when going through a difficult time, such as when you are grieving the loss of a loved one.

Samantha was a dreamer. Sometimes people that have problems with the root chakra are not grounded firmly on this earth. In order to make life more tolerable, they often remove themselves to a dream land. Sometimes this is something they learn to do at a very young age. They aren't particularly happy, and they yearn for better times, but they prefer to dream rather than gather the energy to do something about their circumstances. Clematis can help people put their dreams to action and take an active interest in the world around them.

The root chakra resonates with the colour red. Wearing red can be helpful when you need to strengthen this chakra. People that have fast spinning root chakras may be particularly drawn to red and see it as a high energy power colour. Merlin snuck a pair of red shoes into Samantha's bag when she was busy dreaming. The shoes will help keep Samantha grounded and will boost the energy of her root chakra. They will help her draw energy from the earth, and feel safe and secure. In the movie, The Wizard of Oz, Dorothy clicked her red shoes to bring her back home. Samantha will be able to stay focused and feel like she's at home when she wears her red shoes. Besides, they really did spice up that brown suit!

Chapter Two

Lola had no energy whatsoever. She was exhausted to the very depth of her being. Her feet hurt, her head hurt, and as if that weren't enough, she could feel the beginnings of menstrual cramps.

"Just what I need," she mumbled to her iPhone as she checked the GPS app once again. She wanted to just curl up and cry. It made no sense. Lola was lost. The GPS insisted she was in a vacant parking lot. It was supposed to be the address of a florist shop. More importantly, it was a new client for her father's accounting firm. And yet, even when she carefully wiped the tears from her eyes so as not to mess with her mascara, Lola could see she wasn't in a parking lot, nor was she looking at a flower shop called "Petals and Bows." Instead, she saw an inviting-looking bar.

Not that she needed a bar at the moment that was for sure. Last night's Fuzzy Navels combined with a few too many rum and cokes were contributing to her headache and exhaustion. Lola really hadn't wanted to go out last night. She had planned to stay in her loft apartment to get a start on her marketing class project that was due in two days. But Mary Ellen had insisted she needed Lola to go out with the gang. Since grade seven, Lola had never been able to say no to Mary Ellen. Lola knew if she stayed home, she would have felt so bad for letting Mary Ellen down that she wouldn't have been able to focus on her project anyway. Once she had the first peach schnapps drink, the second, third, and probably fourth had actually been Lola's idea. She didn't seem to be able to control her drinking, just like she couldn't stop eating once she started.

Where she really wanted to be was back home in bed, feeling sick and miserable, but Lola had promised her father she would follow up on this client inquiry. And now she was so tired she couldn't even think straight. How could the GPS be wrong? What was she supposed to do? Maybe someone in the bar would give her directions, she decided.

Lola approached the bar entrance as if on autopilot. She just had to sit down in a soft, cool spot for a moment. As soon as she opened the door, Lola had the feeling she was in a wonderful dream. She braced herself for loud booming music, and instead she heard nothing except the pleasant clinking of wind chimes coming from somewhere. Rather than a smooth lacquered floor, as was typical in the night clubs, Lola was looking at a soft peach carpet that looked about six inches deep. Lola couldn't help herself. She pulled off her high-heeled, pointy slingbacks, and sank her toes deep into the carpet. As her toes stretched and separated from each other, Lola walked towards an elevated armchair-like seat that was positioned in front of the bar like a bar stool. Lola eased her exhausted body into the soft burnt-orange suede, closed her eyes, and felt herself melt.

She felt a presence behind the bar just as she smelled something heavenly. The smell reminded her of being in Sara's house. The two of them used to walk home together from elementary school. Sara's mother often had some kind of wonderful comforting snack ready for them when they got there. They were leftovers or "mistakes" from her catering company. Lola remembered giggling at the huge kitchen table, filling her stomach with treats while she listened to Sara's mother tell stories about her catering business. She was slowly turning her passion into a wonderful business.

"You need today's special."

Lola opened her eyes, surprised to discover the voice came from an unusual looking bartender. And yet, the elderly woman with the long grey braids seemed the perfect owner for the establishment. Her purple plaid flannel shirt looked as comfortable as the setting, and her green eyes portrayed a wisdom that Lola had never seen before.

She placed a bowl of what looked like vanilla pudding in front of Lola. Too tired to register that the desert wasn't a typical bar special, she instead measured the calories and considered the ingredients. "Isn't that an awful lot of lactose?"

The Wise Woman raised one dark eyebrow, a gesture Lola envied and had never been able to perfect despite hours in front of the mirror. "Oh, are you lactose intolerant?"

"No, not at all, in fact I love milk." Lola was surprised to discover that fact, even as she said it. She hoped she hadn't offended the Wise Woman in some way. "It's just that all my friends say lactose is bad for you, so I kind of stay away from it." As she said that, Lola realized how that dumb that sounded, and how good the pudding looked. The Wise Woman passed Lola a spoon.

The pudding was soft and soothing and it seemed to fill her with energy and lift her headache. "Wow, this is amazing!" Lola said. "I was just so exhausted. I feel like I could just sit here and cry. I can't figure out how my directions could be so wrong. I'm too exhausted to even look at this

GPS map anymore. I just want to sleep forever, and not think about anything." Lola yawned and supported her head with one hand, her elbow resting on the smooth bar surface while she continued to spoon in pudding with the other hand.

"You could use some Olive."

Expecting the type of olive you put in a cocktail martini and unsure how that would help anything, Lola was surprised to see the Wise Woman pour some clear liquid into a shot glass and set it in on the bar in front of her.

"It's the Bach Flower essence, Olive. Olive can help restore your strength."

"Oh, sweet. An energy drink." Lola was no stranger to the highs of Red Bull and used them on a regular basis to kick-start the morning after a night of intense studying or partying.

"Bach Flower essences are quite a bit different than that," the Wise Woman said. "They are made from the essence of certain flowers or trees and they very subtly help balance your emotions. Rather than adding something to your body, like caffeine or other stimulants, Olive helps work with your natural healing systems. Olive helps your body find the strength from within to restore your sense of vitality and interest in life. Taking Olive can help you listen to your inner guidance so you recognize what your body needs."

"Cheers to that!" Lola downed the liquid like a shooter, and was surprised to discover it didn't burn or leave any aftertaste. In fact, it tasted like water. "I need something to keep me going, that's for sure. I really don't have the time to listen to my body right now. Sometimes I don't even know how I feel. Maybe when I finish my degree I'll have time to go on a vacation or something. But right now, life is really hectic." The Wise Woman nodded with a type of understanding that inspired Lola to tell her story. Lola told the Wise Woman how she was trying to finish her business degree, with a major in accounting, so she could eventually take over the family business from her father. She was also working part-time for his company so she could "learn the ropes" and so her father could save the company some money. Lola explained how she was also helping out at the woman's shelter. She got involved with the shelter when a friend took the position of director and needed volunteers to help with crisis counselling, babysitting, and odd jobs around the place. Lola had taken the training and felt a responsibility to keep up with the twenty hours a month she had agreed to initially, even though the shelter now had a large compliment of volunteers. The counselling seemed to come naturally to her. Lola often used the listening skills when she dropped everything she was doing to meet with her younger sister. Her sister went through one crisis after another. Lola's friends also relied on her crucial life and relationship advice. Lola was so busy helping friends deal with their relationships that she really didn't have much time for her own. Boyfriends seemed to come and go like new fashion trends. This led to more bar hopping in search of a soul mate, while making some bad choices along the way. Too much drinking seemed to lead to too many one-night stands that left Lola feeling hollow inside and unsure about where she was headed.

 A sleek black cat seemed to appear out of nowhere on top of the counter and pitter-pattered toward her. He sniffed at the empty bowl of pudding for a moment, and was about to lick it clean when the Wise Woman scolded him: "Merlin!" Displeased, he jumped into Lola's lap and settled there.

 The warmth of his body eased her burgeoning menstrual

cramps. She knew that she would be spending a night in bed with a hot water bottle and pain relievers to get through another difficult period. The very thought of it made her stomach cramp even more. She realized the soon-to-be-due marketing project wasn't going to get done if she was sick in bed.

The Wise Woman placed another shot glass of liquid in front of Lola.

"More Olive?" Lola asked. "The last one actually helped me feel less tired, so this would be good because I really can't stop right now."

The Wise Woman shook her head and her thick grey braids swayed with the motion. "This is a different Bach flower essence. This one is Oak."

Having felt an improvement in her mood with the first shot, and never one to turn down a second drink, Lola downed the Oak as well.

The Wise Woman watched Lola closely. "Oak is for people that are normally strong and reliable. Oak people are often the strength of their family, or the pillar in their group of friends. They seem to possess enormous endurance, managing to do everything for everybody. Oak people keep going no matter what, and often ignore how tired they really are. But, like the Oak tree, the Oak person often has so many branches that reach out to help and support others that they tend to become empty inside. They lose their inner core to others, and when they become drained, they tend to suddenly crash, and become depressed. They become frustrated and stressed. If they continue to ignore their feelings, Oak people sometimes develop kidney problems, reproductive problems, fatigue, tension headaches and high blood pressure."

"Hmmm ... sounds a bit like me." Lola rubbed her temple, trying to release the knot of tension.

The Wise Woman started to polish the countertop. "Like Olive, Oak can help you recognize what your body is trying to tell you. It can help you relax. It will help you recognize when you need to take time to look after yourself, so there is still something left of you to help others."

Lola suddenly remembered what she was supposed to be doing. "Oh geez, my father will freak that haven't met with the new client!"

"Do meetings with new clients make you feel good?"

Merlin interrupted his gentle purring to shake his head indignantly as Lola's teardrop landed right between his ears. "No," she whispered.

Once the truth was out, the rest of the story poured from her.

"I hate accounting, and bookkeeping, and all that boring stuff." She sniffed. Lola seemed to gather strength and sat up in her chair to tell her story. She felt like she had no choice but to take over the family business. It seemed like it had been expected of her. Ever since she was a little girl, she had enjoyed spending Saturday mornings in her father's office. The whole family thought she loved the business, when the attraction had been the office supplies and feeling close to her Dad. Lola remembered how she used all the coloured markers and highlighters to draw pictures. She loved to spread out on the floor. She listened to the business schemes and stories of how people were making money, or using their money. She liked hearing the stories of how small bakery shops, clothing stores, or jewellery businesses had "taken off" so they needed her father's sound advice. Lola had been plodding through her accounting major because she felt it was her duty. She couldn't let her father down. She already felt guilty at how hard he worked to build a business he intended to hand over to her. She did really like her marketing classes. She wished she could major in that.

"Oh man, my marketing project," Lola wailed. "I have no idea what I'm even going to do it on. I should have worked on it last night but I always feel guilty if I turn my friends down, especially Mary Ellen. When we were in high school, if I didn't look after her, she would always get in trouble. It has always been my job to make sure things go okay for her, although I can never really get it right, and it seems I'm always doing things that hurt her." The rest of her words were lost in a Kleenex as Lola blew her nose and dabbed away her tears.

Another shot glass appeared as quickly as the box of Kleenexes had materialized. As she drank the liquid, Lola marvelled at the way the Wise Woman seemed able to make things appear from nowhere.

"That one was Pine," she explained. "Pine is helpful for people that are full of guilt and think that everything that goes wrong in the world is their fault. Pine works on a pretty deep layer. Sometimes it is helpful for people that have suppressed their desires and life purpose because of what someone else wants. It can help with the guilt of not fulfilling parental desires."

"I know what I really want to do." Lola leaned forward in her chair. "I want to open my own business. I have dreamed about it for years. I can see it now, '"Lola's Lingerie'." She highlighted the title with her thumb and index finger as though it was spelled out in the air. "I want to design fancy underwear using all kinds of colours. I want women to feel good wearing soft, quality fabric next to their skin. I want them to know that they have a secret from the world under their business suits, grubby jeans, work-out gear, or uniforms. Unless they want to show them off." Lola giggled. "You know what? That's what I'm going to do my marketing project on. I'm going to create the business plan for an exclusive lingerie store. I can't wait to start working on it. I already have it all mapped out in my head anyway. And maybe, when it's finished, I'll show it to my father."

Feeling much better, Lola gently lifted Merlin from her lap, and excused herself to visit the restroom before leaving.

When she returned, instead of a bill by her empty bowl and shot glasses, there was a small black velvet box decorated with a shiny, satin purple and pink bow. Lola lifted the lid to discover, gently wrapped in tissue paper, a pair of silk orange high cut panties, artfully trimmed with soft lace.

"Oh, they are so perfect!" Lola exclaimed, feeling her heart and stomach bubble with love and energy. "Where did you find these?"

Wise Woman smiled. Merlin chewed the end of the bow. "When I took over this place, there was still some inventory in the back room, left over from the last business. "

"Thank you so much for everything." Lola slid her shoes back on and packed her present in her bag. I better go create my future."

Her hand on the door handle, Lola turned back towards the bar. "By the way, what went wrong for the previous business?"

Wise Woman considered the answer as she dried the shot glasses. "Apparently they were busy. It's a good location, and they had high cash flow, but they folded due to cash management issues. It was a bit of an image problem too. Most people thought it was a flower shop, not a lingerie store."

"Petals and Bows!" the Wise Woman and Lola said in unison.

"Well I guess I don't have to feel guilty about missing an appointment!" Lola said. Then, she smiled and walked into the sunshine.

A Note from the Wise Woman

The concerns that Lola brought to the Sweet Shack and Bach Bar were centered on the second or sacral chakra. This chakra, found in the navel area of the body, is focused on creativity and independence.

The sacral chakra usually develops between eight and fourteen years of age. This is a time when children begin to make their own decisions. They typically become independent from parents and others, and find their paths in life. If children are not allowed to develop a sense of independence, they often don't discover their internal motivations for behaviour. They may suffer later on in life. Difficulties with friends, such as an over adherence to peer pressure, or manipulative friends or caregivers can stunt growth in this chakra as well. If this chakra spins too fast, the person may become manipulative, a fantasist, or they may experience addictions. A blocked sacral chakra may be evidenced in an over-sensitive, self-critical person who, like Lola, harbours a lot of guilt. People that are working through or developing this chakra may find they experience both extremes. This is typical pre-teen and teenager behaviour. Once this chakra is well-developed, a person understands their personal internal drives and reacts accordingly. They become trusting, expressive, creative, and attuned to their feelings.

Merlin loves Vanilla Cardamom pudding. We made it when we sensed Lola was on her way because both vanilla and cardamom resonate with the sacral chakra. Vanilla has a long history of sensuality and can be very helpful in awakening the senses. It is also mildly addictive because it increases adrenaline, so it can be an energy booster as well. Merlin is definitely addicted!

The Bach flowers that particularly address emotional imbalances connected to the sacral chakra include Olive, Oak and Pine.

As Lola discovered, Olive can help restore energy when you are exhausted to the point of tears. Olive can be very helpful if you have been going through a difficult period of your life.

Like Olive, Oak also helps restore energy when you are feeling exhausted, especially to the point where you are feeling depressed. Lola is so busy trying to do things for everybody else that she has become empty on the inside. Because of difficulties in the sacral chakra, she has lost sight of how she really feels. Oak will help her take a look at herself and recognize the signals her body is sending her.

Lola's interactions with both her family and friends have left her grappling guilt and self-blame. This often develops over time when personal desires have been hidden or suppressed. Lola no longer knows what she really wants and fluctuates between going along with her friends' desires, and trying to meet the desires of her father. Somewhere in between, she has become confused as to what her emotions and desires are, and tends to feel guilty no matter what she does. Pine will help her as she works through discovering her own motivations, and realizes her personal desires.

The sacral chakra resonates with the colour orange.

Wearing orange can be helpful if you need to boost this chakra. A lot of pre-teens are really drawn to this colour. It matches the emotions they are feeling. Many adults find orange a difficult color to wear, particularly if they have blocked their sexuality to some degree. It was Merlin's idea to present Lola with orange underwear. He knew that wearing orange close to the sacral chakra's location would help her. He also really liked her business idea and wanted her to foster that idea. Merlin hopes Lola will start to make undergarments in all the chakra colors. He also hopes she will send someone else for Vanilla Cardamom pudding!

Chapter Three

Simone had no idea where she was and couldn't decide what to do. This wasn't a part of town where she normally sold properties. Although this address was supposed to be vacant according to her MLS property sheets, which showed it as a potential building site, there was an establishment there. She had assured her client that this would be the perfect location for him to expand his franchise chain. Maybe she would call him and meet him at the second location on her list instead. Yet, this one would be perfect and he had been very excited about it. How could there already be a building there?

"No wonder I didn't want to get out of bed today," Simone mumbled as she retrieved her cell phone from her soft, black leather briefcase. She had bought the briefcase as a present to herself to celebrate her last successful closing. It had screamed, "I belong to a powerful, successful and a no-nonsense person!" to her from the store window. Now she wasn't sure about that as she dug around in it, trying to find her phone. Maybe she should have picked the brown one that had all the organizing pockets instead. She had spent so much time in the store trying to decide that in the end, she had felt pressured and just asked the salesperson what she thought. Simone ended up with the most expensive one.

She dug out some Rolaids and popped a couple of them

while she scanned the address book on her phone for her client's number. She hesitated. Maybe that wasn't the right thing to do. Maybe she should just wait for him and let him decide what he wanted to do. As Simone chewed the antacids, she realized she hadn't eaten anything today. The offending establishment looked like a bar of some sort. They would serve food in there. Maybe she would go order something to eat while she waited. Simone wasn't sure if she wanted breakfast or lunch. Instead of deciding between them, she selected her client's name from the address book and started to dial. When the call didn't go through, she realized that she didn't have reception. Well, decision made, Simone thought. There was nothing to do but go into the bar and wait.

Now that the decision had been made for her, Simone confidently strode toward the bar. She pushed open the heavy oak doors and appraised the quality of the wood. The craftsmanship suggested it was a heritage building, which increased the property value significantly. As she discreetly adjusted her suit pants and wondered how they had gotten so loose, she glanced around and tried to decide where to sit. She had intended to position herself by the window to keep an eye out for her client, but she realized there were no chairs or tables other than the bar stools. They were positioned exactly where they must have been seventy years ago. As she sat down, Simone was already writing up the listing in her head: "Perfectly restored saloon-style bar just waiting for the right bartender."

Simone was expecting a beer-belly cowboy, complete with cowboy hat and handlebar moustache, to walk through the saloon doors from what must have been the kitchen. Instead, a gray haired woman in plaid flannel shirt, jeans, and moccasin slippers appeared. Simone felt a twinge of excitement. Maybe this was the original owner. That would be a wonderful selling feature. And surely, at her wise-old age, she was looking to get out of the business. Simone could sell this place and make a killing.

As Simone was digging for her business cards, the Wise Woman set a yellow glass dessert bowl in front of her. "You need today's special. Pavlova."

"I haven't quite decided if I'm hungry or not," Simone replied as she looked at her watch. "I was thinking I should eat breakfast, but then again it is closer to lunch time. Mind you, if this is what you suggest . . ."

As Simone struggled to decide, a sleek black cat jumped from a rough, wooden beam above her head, landed on the top of the bar, and then hopped to the bar stool beside her. He settled in to watch her with his intense yellow eyes. Simone was a little unnerved by the presence of a cat in an eating establishment. She was trying to decide how she would approach the subject of his removal when the Wise Woman set a shot glass filled with a clear liquid down beside the pavlova.

According to Simone's broker, one of the first rules of the real estate business was to appear in sync with your potential client. Meaning, if they offered you coffee, you drank it. If they offered you a shot glass at eleven-thirty in the morning, you drank it. Simone braced for the burn, wondering how many Rolaids she had left, and swung back the liquid in her best imitation of an old time saloon drinker. She was pleasantly surprised to discover there was no burn. It tasted like water. Maybe the bartender was cutting her costs by watering down the drinks. Not a bad business strategy, if you aren't relying on repeat customers.

"That's a shot of the Bach flower essence Scleranthus," the Wise Woman said. "Scleranthus can help with indecision. Indecision comes from trying to make choices by using only your intellect, and not listening to your intuition. When you aren't feeling that balance, it's difficult to make decisions on simple things. It's hard to even decide on things like what you want to eat."

"I think I understand that." Simone dragged her spoon around the bowl to get every last bit of the sweet meringue, the tangy lemon, and the cool whipped cream. "This pavlova definitely feels right. I sometimes drive myself crazy trying to make what should be the simplest decisions. For instance, this morning I couldn't figure out whether I should wear this suit, or my hunter green knit dress. I kept thinking the suit was a power statement, but people tell me the dress looks really good on me, and maybe it seems less intimidating. I just kept going back and forth. I even found myself asking my angel fish, Puddles, which one I should wear!"

The Wise Woman laughed. "Did Puddles answer?"

Simone smiled, and wagged her empty spoon at the Wise Woman. "I think he voted for the dress but it's hard to hear him through the bubbles. I decided that fish don't really understand the fashion world, so I eventually went with what I last tried on."

"Would you like some more pavlova?" the Wise Woman asked.

"I would love more pavlova," Simonereplied. "You know, I actually am quite decisive in the big areas of my life. A promotion at work feels right to me."

The Wise Woman handed over another bowl of pavlova and settled in to listen to Simone's story.

Once she started on the subject of work, Simone seemed

to talk faster. She explained that she couldn't understand why things weren't happening faster for her. She put everything she had into her career, like staying up late to search listings, getting up early to meet with clients, and taking courses to get her broker's license. She usually took all the pictures for her properties herself, and even designed the brochures and the website listings rather than use the support staff. She felt that it was the only way to really get it right. It seemed that by the time she explained what she wanted to someone else, she could have just done it herself. One of the aspects of real estate that she really liked was that for the most part, she could work alone. That way, she could set her own pace and not bother with lunch hour, or coffee breaks, or fixed work hours. Instead, she could just focus on work all the time.

Simone admitted that lately she was experiencing a lot of heartburn and digestive problems. She jumped up to show the Wise Woman her loose-fitting pants that only a couple of weeks ago had fit perfectly. She knew she was losing weight because she was surviving on nothing but coffee and often forgot to eat. Considering she had less than one hundred pounds on a five foot six frame, she really couldn't afford to lose more weight.

While she talked, Simone dug frantically through her briefcase to find the Rolaids. In the process, she scattered a stack of files all over the oak floor, causing the cat to leap up on the bar counter in disgust. As she bent to retrieve the documents, she smashed her head on the edge of the bar, which brought tears to her eyes. Thankful to have something to do with her hands, and wanting to divert attention from her clumsiness, Simone quickly downed the contents of another shot glass that had appeared in front of her.

"That was a few drops of the Bach Flower essence, Impatiens," the Wise Woman said, speaking slowly and distinctly in a calming voice. "Impatiens is helpful when you become irritated when the world seems to be moving too slowly. Impatiens can help you relax a bit so you can cope with irritating problems. Impatiens can help ease tension and pain."

Simone gently rubbed her head while she considered this information.

"Sometimes, I am kind of afraid to relax," Simone admitted. "I'm scared that if I stop, I won't be able to start again."

She explained she often stayed up late working on projects because she knew she wouldn't want to get out of bed in the morning. She felt like she couldn't face the work that had to be done. She felt tired before her feet even touched the floor, and the thought of getting dressed and facing another "tire-kicking" client made her feel weary. She felt she just couldn't get started. Instead of getting up in the morning when the alarm went off, she laid in bed thinking about all the things she didn't want to do.

"Is there a Bach flower for that Monday morning feeling?" Simone kept an eye on the cat, who had returned to see if there was any pavlova left in her bowl.

"You catch on quickly," the Wise Woman said as she handed Simone another shot glass. "That's Hornbeam. People need Hornbeam sometimes when they are suffering from overwork or a lack of variety in their life. Hornbeam is for people who are mentally exhausted. The type of people who can benefit from Hornbeam usually get everything done, but every once in a while they start to doubt their abilities. It can help you realize that you do have the strength and the ability to face the day so that life becomes more enjoyable again."

"Speaking of facing the day, I better go find my client."

Simone stacked her bowls and spoons and stood up, slinging her briefcase over her shoulder, and buttoned up her suit jacket.

"You know, when I first came in here, I thought that I might be able to convince you to list this place," Simone admitted. "But I'm going to find something else for my client instead. I think I might need to come back here now and again."

"I think you left this the last time." The Wise Woman handed a thin bright yellow belt to Simone with a smile. "This might help that "pants issue" you're having."

Simone was so thankful for the belt that she didn't register what the Wise Woman had said until she was back out on the street. She turned to go back and explain she had never been in the bar before, but the lot was vacant again. She smiled at a particularly bright patch of goldenrod that was growing where she could have sworn she had been sitting a few minutes ago. Rather than analyze what had happened, Simone decided to just go with the flow and crossed the street to check for cell phone coverage.

A Note from the Wise Woman

The concerns that Simone brought to the Sweet Shack and Bach Bar were centered on the third or solar chakra. Located between the belly button and the base of the sternum, this chakra is also referred to as the naval chakra. The focus of this chakra is on personal power, willpower, and perseverance.

The third chakra typically develops between fourteen and twenty-one years of age. Usually, by then, you have moved through the root chakra development. You have a sense of belonging. You also have usually moved through the relationship aspect of the sacral chakra and have developed independence. Growth continues through the third chakra, where you develop the personal power that brings you a sense of uniqueness. Development of this chakra is achieved when there is a balance between the logical left side and the intuitive right side of the brain.

If this chakra spins too fast, the person may appear to be angry, controlling, judgmental, and condescending. They are often workaholics. If this chakra is blocked, the person may appear insecure, and may constantly seek the reassurance of others. Once this chakra is fully developed and balanced, the person will have respect for both him or herself and others, and will be spontaneous, uninhibited, and confident. When balanced, one's head does not overrule one's heart and vice versa.

Pavlova takes a lot of time and patience to make, but it isn't at all difficult. We made it for Simone because the yellow lemon resonates with the third chakra. The process of making it can be helpful when your third chakra is spinning a bit too fast. It encourages you to slow down and be more patient.

The Bach Flowers that are suited to the emotional problems of an unbalanced third chakra are Scleranthus, Impatiens, and Hornbeam.

Simone was struggling to make decisions about simple things like what to wear, or eat. This is a common problem when there are blockages in the solar chakra. Simone was spending too much time considering the intellectual side of things and was ignoring her feelings. Scleranthus can help Simone balance her emotions and find the mix between logic and feeling. Once these two ways of thinking are balanced, decision-making becomes much easier.

Impatiens is the Bach flower that can help with the workaholic nature of an unbalanced third chakra. Simone's third chakra was spinning pretty fast. She expected others to maintain the same pace, and became frustrated when they weren't keeping up. When Simone became over-controlling and wanted to do everything herself, rather than waiting for others, she found that Impatiens helped to balance her. Then she could slow down and balance work with other aspects of her life. People needing Impatiens often find themselves taking some "knocks to the head" as they are prone to accidents borne out of haste and impatience.

Using the logical side of your brain as much as Simone was doing can lead to severe mental weariness. That's why we gave her the Bach Flower Hornbeam. Simone wasn't listening to her heart, only to her head, and was taking herself beyond the limits of her physical abilities. When she did stop to lie down, her body didn't want to get up again. Hornbeam will help her balance the need to overwork so that she can set her priorities and get the appropriate things done. Her sense of enthusiasm will be restored.

The solar chakra resonates with the colour yellow. Wearing yellow can be helpful if you are feeling insecure and lack confidence. It can help boost the solar chakra and restore energy. Too much yellow can feel overwhelming, however, as it is a powerful colour. Merlin suggested I give Simone a thin yellow belt. He wanted to address her third chakra without encouraging it to spin too fast. A yellow shirt would help boost the chakra if it was blocked, but would have been too much for Simone. In her case, we think she will slow down and listen to her body's needs. Until then, it seems like she will need that belt to hold up her pants!

Chapter Four

Jeanne was worried about everyone and everything. Ever since her daughter Angelica had been little, she had resisted wearing winter boots. Positive that she would catch her death if her feet weren't warm and dry, Jeanne had made her daughter put on boots. Every year, she bought boots for her, even if they never were worn. Of all her four children, Angelica had always been the difficult one and the one Jeanne worried about the most.

"Lord knows, none of them were easy," Jeanne mumbled through frozen lips as she stamped her sensible mukluks partly to keep warm, and partly in frustration. She pulled her knee length, puffy beige coat, tight at the throat to keep the wind from blowing right through her. The last thing she needed was an asthma attack out in the middle of the street, in who-knows-where. Not that anyone would even notice her missing until supper wasn't on the table. Michelle, her daughter-in-law, had suggested that Jeanne check this particular store for Angelica's boots. Michelle said she had ordered online from this place and got a pair of fashionable boots in the wide size that both she and Angelica required. No way was Jeanne going to trust the internet with her credit card number, so she had Michelle give her the address. Now, three bus transfers later, she was supposed to be in front of a shoe store. It looked more like a bar for crying out loud! Wasn't this just what she needed: to freeze to death outside a bar in a bad part of town, trying to find boots for a daughter who likely wasn't going to appreciate them anyway? In fact, Angelica was teaching English in Hong Kong for a year, and, if she even came home for Christmas, she would probably run around in sneakers in the middle of winter.

Jeanne felt the tightness in her chest signalling the beginning of an attack. "Maybe she'll come home for my funeral," she murmured as she pushed open the door of the bar. Jeanne figured that she wasn't likely to get any help in a bar, but going in seemed better than freezing to death, or dying of an asthma attack, alone on the street. Maybe, she could get a glass of lemon juice to ease the constriction.

Jeanne stamped the snow off her boots on the welcome mat. The warm air immediately fogged the lenses of her silver framed glasses so that she could only make out shapes, as she blindly made her way towards the bar. She pulled a tissue from deep in the pocket of her coat and wiped her glasses dry. She expected to see pathetic male patrons drooling over spilled beer, but she was surprised to find herself the only customer in what appeared to be a clean, comfortable establishment. She realized that the bar stool she had selected really looked and felt more like a kitchen chair with a cushioned back and simple, easy to clean upholstery. Rather than the round seat of a typical bar stool, the chair provided ample space for her hips, which seemed to be bigger as of late. She settled in, placing her brown shoulder purse on the surprisingly clean floor.

Jeanne realized that the bar appeared to be more like a kitchen. The soothing smell of chocolate baking was making her feel at home. When the bartender appeared, balancing three plates while backing through the swinging saloon door, Jeanne noticed that the woman looked a lot like her mother did in her later years. Although Jeanne's mother had always worn her long grey hair tightly constricted in a bun, Jeanne suspected it would have looked similar if she had allowed it to relax in the simple braids that the bartender wore. And yet, there was something about the wisdom in the bartender's eyes that made her seem unique.

"You'll be needing today's special." It was clearly a statement, not a question. The Wise Woman set one of the green plates with an individual-sized molten chocolate cake in front of Jeanne.

Jeanne swallowed to prevent herself from drooling over the dark chocolate mound that smelled incredible. It was so beautifully presented with its heart shaped sugar decoration, and a dollop of whipped cream. She gently pushed the plate away to avoid temptation. "Sorry, my doctor has me on a gluten-free diet to try and control my allergies and asthma."

"Eat to your heart's content, my dear. This recipe is gluten-free." The Wise Woman handed Jeanne a heavy antique ivory-handled fork.

The whipped cream melted and settled into the cracks in the cake as chocolate lava from the inside oozed onto the plate when Jeanne pierced it with her fork. She scooped lava and cake onto the fork and closed her eyes as she savoured the bittersweet, pure chocolate taste.

"Amazing; even my sister Charlene, the chocolate connoisseur would approve," Jeanne said.

This whole experience was much more like something that would happen to Charlene. Charlene was the lucky one in the family. While Jeanne was scraping to save pennies and buying unlucky lottery tickets, Charlene was finding fifty dollar bills in parking lots, and getting design contracts handed to her. Of course, as the younger sister, Charlene had always been taken care of. It was Jeanne that looked after their aging parents, while Charlene went away to design school. Jeanne struggled to keep up the traditions, raise four children, and ensure that their mother had grandchildren close to her. Jeanne made sure that she was always available, should either of their parents need her, while Charlene gallivanted around, living the glamorous single life of a career woman without a care in the world. Jeanne was the one who always got short changed by life, while Charlene sailed through it all on the winds of luck.

Feeling her chest tighten and her throat constrict, Jeanne reached for the shot glass that had appeared in front of her, grateful for anything liquid. As she tossed it back, she realized that it tasted like water.

"That's a shot of the Bach Flower essence, Willow." The Wise Woman seemed to hear Jeanne's questioning thoughts. "Willow is helpful when you are feeling a bit 'hard done by' in life. When you are feeling victimized by your circumstances and resentful of others' success, Willow can help you find balance. Willow helps people forgive and forget past injustices so they don't feel like victims. It can restore a sense of control, so you can enjoy life and create your own destiny."

"Control, wouldn't that be nice!" Jeanne muttered.

She watched a black cat slink around the corner of the bar, licking his lips. She could have sworn he smelled like the dark chocolate color he was. Jeanne wondered why her acute allergies hadn't been triggered as she watched him curl up on her coat in the chair beside her.

"He's looking a little thin," Jeanne commented as she

stared at the cat.

The Wise Woman chuckled. "Oh, don't worry about Merlin. He's better fed than most cats, I would say."

Jeanne sighed. "Sometimes I think I just worry too much."

"Hmm . . ." The Wise Woman picked up a knitting project and settled in to listen, the needles making clicking sounds while Merlin purred in chocolate bliss.

"I just really can't stop worrying about Angelica, for instance." As she thought of her daughter, Jeanne went to grasp her St. Christopher necklace. He was the patron saint of travellers. Feeling nothing there, she remembered the necklace had broken that morning. It had got tangled in the worn lace neckline of her flannel nightgown. When she had pulled it over her head, the necklace chain broke. Her neck felt bare and exposed without the protective trinket.

Jeanne explained how she had worried when the chain broke, that it might mean something had happened to Angelica, and she had wanted to phone her to make sure she was alright. But Frank, Jeanne's husband, had insisted that the phone call would wake Angelica up, given the time difference. Frank said she was just being superstitious. But Hong Kong was so far away. Anything could be going on there. There was so much to worry about in a foreign country like muggings, kidnappings, and bombings. Angelica never paid enough attention to her surroundings. She didn't think about practical things like eating right, or checking for expiry dates, or avoiding chicken in dirty restaurants, or making sure she had an extra sweater in case the weather suddenly turned cold. The last time Jeanne talked to her she thought Angelica sounded like she might be catching a cold. There was always that bird flu virus to think about.

Jeanne worried that the Wise Woman was going to drop a stitch or two just leaving her knitting in the middle of a row to pour another shot. Merlin hopped up on the bar and eyed the ball of yarn, as if considering whether or not he might unravel it.

The Wise Woman set the shot glass in front of Jeanne and moved the knitting away from Merlin's tempted paws. "This is a shot of Red Chestnut. It helps when you are overly concerned for the welfare of others. It's natural for mothers to worry about their children. It's part of the job description." She smiled at Merlin and stroked him from head to tail while he leaned into her hand and wove himself around her. "But when that worry becomes all-consuming and you start thinking that something minor will turn into something serious, Red Chestnut can help. It can help you care for others without feeling anxious. It can allow you to relax, helping only when asked, allowing you to let go when others need to find their own way."

Jeanne drank the liquid in one gulp, anxious to feel the balance that the Wise Woman promised. "It's true that Angelica doesn't always want my help, that's for sure." Jeanne dug a Kleenex out from her sweatshirt sleeve and blew her nose. "Sometimes, I just feel so unappreciated." Jeanne sniffed, put the Kleenex back, smoothed her sweatshirt sleeves and brushed some chocolate crumbs from her corduroy pants.

It was so good to have listening ears. She explained the whole story to the Wise Woman and Merlin. When Angelica had left home and gone so far away, Jeanne had felt lost and alone. Having spent so many years taking care of everyone, she really didn't know what to do. She had always made sure that meals were homemade and nutritious. She had looked after her parents, her children, and many of the neighbourhood children. There were always cookies fresh from the oven, and stews in the winter. Clothes were always washed and ironed. Jeanne had made sure that lunches were made, the house was clean, and that everyone had their school projects done. She had made birthday celebrations into elaborate affairs with homemade piñatas and that special, perfect present. But it seemed that as soon as they could, her children abandoned her. They didn't seem to appreciate the home-cooked meals and all her other efforts. She had imagined they would come for Sunday suppers every week, just as she had taken them to her parents for Sunday meals when her parents had been alive. It was just the way things were supposed to be, no matter what. But her kids seemed to find excuses not to come. Like the boots, for instance. Jeanne would knock herself out looking for boots that Angelica wouldn't even want to wear, say thanks for, or appreciate. Angelica wasn't even sure if she would come home for Christmas!

Jeanne dug in her purse for a fresh stack of Kleenex. When she lifted her head again, Merlin was weaving around a new shot glass at her place, as though he had been the one to set it there.

"That's a shot of Chicory." The Wise Woman removed the empty plates and polished the bar counter while she explained. "Chicory is helpful for strong people, who can be a bit manipulative with their love. It is for people who find it difficult to give without expecting something in return. Sometimes strong-willed people expect others to conform to their values, rather than adopt values of their own. Chicory can help you love unconditionally, accept others and allow them to live their own lives. It can help you realize you don't need assurance from others to know that you are worthy of love. It can help you to be more sensitive to what others really need." She paused and stared at Jeanne in a somewhat unnerving, soul-baring way. "It can also help you accept yourself."

"Well, that's telling it like it is," Jeanne said, but she smiled. "I appreciate your honesty, though. Sometimes I can be a little possessive, I know that. My mother was the same way and every so often, I need to be reminded that there are other ways of doing things besides my own."

Jeanne looked down at her mukluks that dripped melted snow onto the floor. "You know, Angelica sent me a pair of silly yellow-and-green flowered flip-flops a couple of weeks ago in the mail. They are totally impractical. They have an annoying thong between your toes. You really can't walk in them. They came with a letter suggesting that instead of buying her winter boots and clothes she didn't need this year, I should buy a plane ticket to Hong Kong and visit her after Christmas. She said she could show me the sights and we could celebrate Chinese New Year. I was mad that she wouldn't want to come home for Christmas. Maybe I should rethink that. I have always dreamed of having the freedom to travel. Maybe that's where Angelica gets it from. When she was little, we used to look at travel magazines together and dream up stories."

Jeanne stood up and realized for the first time, she didn't feel the constriction in her chest.

"This has been really nice. It's been a long time since I spent the afternoon chatting with a couple of friends. Almost supper time though. Maybe I'll just take home some Chinese take-out the kids are always raving about."

Jeanne picked up her coat. On the chair lay a teardrop-shaped, malachite necklace on a leather string. "Someone must have left this." Jeanne admired the swirls of green shades on the solid piece of crystal. "How beautiful!"

"Merlin left that there for you," the Wise Woman said. "Wear it until you get that St. Christopher necklace repaired."

Jeanne put the necklace on. The stone rested over her heart, making her feel warm and comforted. Merlin followed her to the door and settled in the front window. She opened the door into the snow and embraced the cool air, rather than bracing for it. She headed for the bus stop, and as she turned to wave, the bar was gone. Near the spot she would have expected to see Merlin, she saw a mother doe with two fawns. The fawns were munching on some late fall grass they had dug out of the snow. The mother lifted her head and made eye contact with Jeanne. Sensing no danger, the mother bent her head to retrieve more grass. Jeanne touched her new necklace and carried on with her journey.

A Note from the Wise Woman

Jeanne arrived at the Sweet Shack and Bach Bar with concerns rooted in the heart chakra. This fourth chakra is located in the heart area of the chest. The main issues of this chakra involve love and relationships. Unlike lower chakras that focus on interactions with others, the goal of the fourth chakra is to develop love and acceptance of self regardless of external influences.

Most people are focused on heart chakra development between the ages of twenty-one and twenty-eight years. By this time, if you have worked through your place in society, and discovered your personal power, you start to become more forgiving and are able to relate compassionately with others. For many, this is the time when they choose someone they wish to spend their life with. Many people may transition from the self-absorbed nature of self-discovery and career advancement to a focus on parenting and nurturing roles.

If the heart chakra spins too fast, the person is often possessive with his or her love and withholds emotionally in order to punish. Conditional love is often overly dramatic and can be destructive in nature. If the heart chakra is blocked, the person may feel unworthy of love. He or she may experience fears of rejection, love too much, or feel sorry for themselves.

Merlin and I chose molten chocolate cakes for Jeanne's heart chakra issues. Although green vegetables resonate with the heart chakra as well, they don't make for good desserts! Luckily, chocolate has strong links with the heart, as well. It is said to be a subtle aphrodisiac because it releases endorphins into our system. We also chose the molten cakes because of the lack of boundaries they represent. The outer cake and the inner core mix and combine in such a way that one isn't quite sure whether one is eating cake or pudding. This lack of boundaries is an issue for the heart chakra to resolve.

The Bach Flowers that are suited to the emotional imbalances experienced in the heart chakra are Willow, Chicory, and Red Chestnut.

When Jeanne first arrived, she was feeling victimized by her circumstances and was feeling sorry for herself. She was feeling resentful of her sister's easy-going life and her children's ability to distance themselves from her. Jeanne was starting to interpret the world as being out to get her when she deserved better. Willow can help Jeanne forget past grudges and injustices so that she can move on to enjoy life. Willow can help her be more accepting and feel in control of her life.

Jeanne's heart chakra was spinning too fast and she had become possessive and conditional in her love. This typical heart chakra reaction can be helped with the Bach flower essence Chicory. People like Jeanne like to keep adult children under their thumb and within their control. Sometimes, they will manifest physical conditions like heart pains or asthma attacks in order to gain attention. This may be something Jeanne inherited from her parents. Rejection, fear, and betrayal can also result in dysfunctional attitudes towards love. Chicory can help people give without expecting anything in return. It can help Jeanne find self-assurance so that she no longer needs other people's approval to feel worthy of love. It will help her regain genuine, nurturing, maternal love. She can live her own life while allowing her children to live theirs.

We gave Jeanne the Bach Flower essence Red Chestnut to address her consuming worries. It is an essence that is often required when the boundaries between parent and child are blurred. Red Chestnut will help Jeanne experience compassion without anxiety.

The heart chakra resonates with the color green. Wearing green or surrounding yourself with the greens of nature can help restore trust and emotional security. Malachite, a green crystal, is often used to help balance this chakra. Merlin chose the necklace so Jeanne could wear this crystal close to her heart chakra and feel peace instead of fear when she thinks of her family.

Chapter Five

Rachael wished she was dreaming. Even the old nightmares would have been better than this fearful reality. She could feel someone watching her, even though she couldn't see anyone. She arranged her car keys in the center of her palm, and poked a key between each finger before she curled her hand into a tight fist. Creating brass knuckles out of car keys was second nature to her.

She walked along the far edge of the sidewalk, distancing herself from any alleyways or buildings where someone might be lurking, ready to grab her purse, or pull her into the darkness. Unlike other city women, Rachael didn't hang her purse across her shoulder to prevent it from being snatched. She chose to leave her purse as an easy grab. She wasn't afraid of her money being stolen as much as she was afraid of being beaten in a struggle. She figured that she would be happy enough to give up her purse if it meant the thief would keep running without hurting her. Maybe she had never completely adjusted to city living, having grown up in a rural area. Rachael's upbringing was living proof that country living wasn't always peaceful, but at least in a small town you knew who the devils were, and where you would find them.

The late afternoon September sun was casting shadows,

so Rachael picked up her pace a bit, thinking about how much she didn't want to be out alone in the dark. When she had volunteered to organize the street youth group's Christmas pageant, she knew the rest of the staff had all breathed a sigh of relief. To them, the pageant was something that had to be done to keep the program funders happy and the grant mandate fulfilled. They all complained about how much time funding issues took away from the real job of social work. Usually Rachael agreed, but pageants were a personal passion and she saw them as a way to really work out some issues with the kids. So when she heard about a comic book store that also sold self-published scripts from local writers, she knew she could find something great to adapt. She had been struggling with a sore throat all week and she figured there was a good chance that she was going to end up home sick with a virus, so it would be a good chance to review the scripts.

When she told the other staff members where she was going, they warned her that it wasn't a great part of town. Many of them had clients around the neighbourhood and said they wouldn't go anywhere near there after dark. Rachael had joked that her farm-fed, six-foot imposing stature would be enough to send any would-be mugger running for the hills. She had joked about wrestling steers before breakfast and they had all left the lunchroom with tears of laughter streaking their mascara.

The fact was that, although Rachael grew up on a dairy farm, no one there had ever wrestled a steer, taking a much gentler approach to bovine management. And although she had taken a ton of self-defence courses, she was still terrified of being attacked. To make matters worse, she was staring at a closed sign in the window of the comic book store. It would be at least forty-five minutes before the bus would return, and she hadn't seen a taxi since she left the office.

Thinking that she heard footsteps behind her, she turned. Instead of seeing a would-be mugger, she noticed an open sign flashing in the window of what looked like a bar. It would probably be safer in there than it was out on the dark street.

"Back to the devil I know," she mumbled as she pushed open the door.

Rachael swallowed past the soreness in her throat as she looked around the bar and thought about how her father's cure for a sore throat, or for anything for that matter, had been a bottle of whiskey, often consumed in a bar like this. And yet, as she looked around, she didn't think that this was the type of place where her father would have felt at home. There were no old "down and outs" drinking, playing cards, smoking and complaining while they slopped beer on the tables or drank straight from the bottle. The bar could only be described as "homey." It looked like a country-style coffee shop. Although Rachael had dragged her father out of a lot of bars, she had never seen blue gingham tablecloths in any of them. The bouquets of bachelor buttons and forget-me-knots looked like the real ones that Rachael used to pick for her grandmother. The glass milk bottle vases that held the flowers caught the sunlight and brightened up the place. Rachael was struck by the smell. She realized it wasn't that of beer-drowned cigarette smoke, cows and sweat, but instead a heavenly smell of mint, chocolate, and fresh baking.

She breathed in deeply, sat her bag on the floor, and sprawled onto a blue velvet bar stool. She crossed her arms on the bar counter, collapsed her forehead on her arms, and felt her back and shoulders melt, only then realizing how tense she had been.

When she heard the heaving, wheezing sound, Rachael thought for a moment she was back in the milking barn.

"Nothing quite like the sound of a cat bringing up a hair ball," she said to the bartender, who looked much more like a hard-working, wise-old, seen-it-all farm wife. In her plaid flannel shirt and loose-fitting, worn jeans she could have been heading in from the cream separator.

The Wise Woman nodded in agreement and sat a plate of warm cheesecake down in front of Rachael. She passed her a fork, just like Rachael's grandmother did millions of times before. "You'll need the special today."

"Peppermint cheesecake." Rachael swallowed to prevent herself from drooling. "This was a special treat for us at Christmas time. One of the church ladies always made this out of candy canes after the Christmas pageant. Coming from dairy country, I think I've had every flavour of cheesecake, but I always associate peppermint with Christmas, even in September."

"I'm sort of getting a jump on the holidays I guess, sort of a trial run of recipes. Couldn't find candy canes anywhere, but I'm rather fond of this chocolate mint version instead. Merlin found it quite helpful apparently." As the Wise Woman spoke, a sleek black cat appeared beside Rachael.

Rachael watched Merlin clean his chest and paws. It seemed as though he owned the place. "Yup, that's what they always do once a hairball comes up."

She immediately blushed as she realized that city folks didn't usually talk about hair balls and cats while eating! Thoughts of the city reminded her of why she had run into the bar in the first place.

"I was so glad to see this place open," Rachael said. "I

was sure that I was about to be mugged, or attacked, or worse. I know I can take care of myself and I am always aware of my surroundings—I have triple locks on my door—but I'm still scared. Maybe it's just part of being a social worker. I just see the world a bit differently."

As she listened, the Wise Woman filled a shot glass and set it in front of Rachael. "Try this. It's a shot of the Bach flower essence Mimulus."

Rachael lifted the glass to her nose and smelled it. The Wise Woman certainly seemed like someone you could trust but Rachael usually drank only from the bottle in bars, and she made sure that she saw the bottle being opened. The shot didn't even smell like alcohol. "I've heard about Bach Flower essences. One of the therapists I often refer clients to uses them in her practice. I've always wondered about trying them, but I've been a little scared."

"That's what Mimulus is for," the Wise Woman replied as Merlin rubbed up against Rachael's shoulder. "It's for people who know that they have a fear of specific things, like the dark, an illness, or getting mugged. These types of people are often artistic and talented but they can be shy. Sometimes they blush easily or they laugh when they're nervous. Mimulus can help you change fear into purposeful action so that you can have control and enjoy a peaceful life."

Rachael wanted to tap the bottom of the glass to make sure she got every single drop. That description sounded so much like her. She gently set the empty shot glass down and cleared her throat to get rid of the lump. Merlin snuggled up against her again. She scratched him behind the ear and stroked his fur while he stretched into her hand. His eyes were wide as they stared up at her wild red hair, as if he were captivated by its colour. Rachael took another bite of the cheesecake and almost purred her satisfaction. It tasted like a strange and wonderful combination of opposites. The warmth of the cake masked the coolness of the mint, and every once in a while the smooth cream of the filling would meet with a hard chunk of peppermint. The mint was very soothing to the throat and seemed to loosen things up so that Rachael really felt like talking.

"You know, no one at work has any idea that I'm scared of anything. All my friends think that I am this tough, brave person who just laughs everything off. I guess I'm a pretty good actress."

The Wise Woman seemed content to just listen to Rachael's story. A stream of sunshine hit the place on the bar counter where Merlin was laying. He purred. When neither of them objected, Rachael continued to talk.

Rachael explained how she had always loved drama class and pageants of any kind. She loved putting on a costume and taking on a role. Once in character, she could perform in front of anyone and everyone. When things weren't good at home, which was a frequent occurrence, she would just escape into another character. In fact, she had gotten good at diverting people's attention and preventing arguments between her parents by putting on an act. She often used what might have been painful childhood stories as fuel for jokes as a way to lighten things up when conflicts started at work, or between friends. As she talked it out, Rachael was shocked to realize that she was really concealing some deep fears and torment behind a facade of laughter and light-heartedness that really wasn't genuine. As she felt the lump in her throat again and tears threatened to flow, she squished her fork into the last crumbs of the cheesecake. With the other hand she reached up and released her ponytail so her wild red mane would hide her face. From around the fuzzy curtain of hair she could see the Wise Woman rise and pour another shot, which she placed by Rachael's plate.

"That's a shot of Agrimony," the Wise Woman explained. "People that need Agrimony often appear carefree and humorous to others, but it's a mask that they wear to hide their real feelings. They try to avoid conflict at all costs, and will often steer the conversation to more harmonious topics. This method of coping can become so entrenched that you aren't even aware that you are doing it. Agrimony can help you communicate your real feelings and accept that life does have a less pleasant side that should be addressed. Then, your cheerfulness can come from a real sense of self-acceptance and inner joy, instead of playing the role of a character. Agrimony may even help with that restlessness that prevents you from sleeping at night."

Rachael didn't question how the Wise Woman knew about the restless nights—it was obvious that she just seemed to "know" things.

She drank the Bach Flower shot. "Sometimes I get up and write when I can't sleep. That's how I wrote most of my screenplay."

Merlin sat up and gently raised his paw to play with the outer frizz of curls that touched her shoulder.

"You wrote a screenplay?"

That was the opening Rachael needed to share her precious project. Rachael straightened her back, and used her hands to emphasize her words. Feeling it best to avoid the widely swinging fork, Merlin leaped to the rafter to watch.

Rachael explained how the musical script was an anti-bullying program she wanted to bring to the schools. As she took Merlin and the Wise Woman through the story line, she described the colourful characters, who took on real-life roles to act out why bullying starts and how it can be stopped in simple, realistic ways that kids could emulate. Rachael described how youth groups could benefit from playing the roles as much as the audience could learn from watching the play. She had incorporated principles of peer teaching and left room for the actors to insert their own thoughts, feelings, and methods into the script, so that no two performances would ever be the same. When she got to the end, she sang the last two lines of the final chorus and took a bow. The Wise Woman clapped her approval and Merlin jumped from his perch to join the excitement.

Almost as quickly as Rachael's enthusiasm came, it suddenly waned. She felt deflated. She returned to the stool and tied her hair back in a ponytail.

"I don't know, do you really think it's any good?" Rachael asked. Without waiting for an answer, she cleared her throat and explained that she really wanted to have the courage to try it out instead of finding another Christmas Pageant script, but she had asked a couple of people at work and they had told her it didn't sound very Christmas-like. They thought it would be hard to pull off and would take a lot of extra time and effort.

The Wise Woman gave Rachael another shot glass.

While Rachael drank, Wise Woman described the benefits of Cerato. "Cerato is for people who don't trust their judgement to make decisions. They know what they want and they have plenty of inner wisdom, but they constantly seek advice from others. They will often follow the misguided opinions of others, rather than trust themselves."

"You know, I have read a lot of scripts, performed and directed a lot of plays, and seen a lot of really crappy anti-bullying programs," Rachael said as she smiled. "I'll be wait'n till the cows come home before I find a really good one. I've got some really great kids in this year's youth group and I know they're ready for something as challenging as my script. I don't care how much time it takes, I'm going to give up this wild goose chase of finding another play and use my own instead."

She gathered her things, placed the empty shot glasses on the blue enamel plate and pushed her mess across the counter as she towered over the bar. "As the church ladies in Dairyland say, you have been a breath of fresh air sent straight from heaven, and I thank you for your hospitality."

Rachael buttoned her coat and looked around to say goodbye to Merlin, but he was nowhere to be found. Disappointed, she said, "Tell Merlin I'm glad his hairball is gone."

"Tell him yourself." The Wise Woman smiled as Merlin came in from the kitchen, proudly dragging a sky-blue cashmere scarf. He placed it by Rachael's feet.

"Oh my goodness, how beautiful!" Rachael exclaimed. She scratched Merlin's ear, retrieved the scarf and held it out to the Wise Woman.

"Oh, no," the Wise Woman said as she shook her head. "That's a present to you from Merlin. I think he wants you to wear it on opening night."

Rachael wrapped the scarf around her throat, pulling her ponytail over top, enjoying the softness of the fabric on her skin as she knotted it. She lingered for just a moment on the threshold, unsure if she wanted to leave the safety of the bar. But then, her bus rolled down the street.

"Oh, there's my bus, thank you, thank you!" she exclaimed as she ran to catch it.

Breathlessly, she sat in the middle of the bus and glanced

back to wave to Merlin and the Wise Woman. Where the bar had been, there was a vacant lot. As Rachael tried to make sense of it all, she saw a light blue balloon float up steadily on a journey to the moon. It seemed to originate from the exact spot where the bar had been. As Rachael watched it go, she considered how light and free the balloon seemed to be. She tightened the scarf as she composed a song about balloons.

A Note from the Wise Woman

Rachael came to visit Merlin and I with issues centered in the throat chakra. This fifth chakra is located centrally at the base of the neck, the throat area. The main issues of this chakra are communication and self-expression. This higher level chakra combines faith and trust with a sense of self developed in the lower chakras, so that you can speak the truth, knowing it comes from a pure inner source. When this chakra is balanced, you find it easy to communicate and you may feel artistically inspired.

This chakra usually develops when a person is between the ages of twenty-eight and thirty-five. Ideally, by this age, people have developed a clear sense of who they are. They understand their strengths and accept their weaknesses. This confidence, combined with compassion from the heart, allows them to speak the truth even if it is not always accepted by others.

If this chakra spins too fast, the individual may seem arrogant, overly talkative, and self-righteous. If this chakra spins too quickly, the person may be more of a talker than a listener and may not be an effective communicator.

On the other hand, childhood traumas or low self-esteem

can block this chakra. In Rachael's case, somewhere along the line, she came to believe that her opinion was not valued. This blocked her chakra, so she holds back from self-expression. She doesn't tell people how she really feels. This type of suppression can cause physical complaints, such as a sore throat or laryngitis. Merlin says that, in cats, it causes hairballs to get stuck!

I made Peppermint Cheesecake for Rachael. Peppermint resonates with this chakra and can be soothing for the throat. As Rachael discovered, the contrasts of the smooth and the hard, and the warm and the cool of this recipe reflect the inconsistent views that people with blocked throat chakras may express. They fluctuate back and forth between other people's contrasting opinions rather than speaking their own thoughts.

The Bach Flowers that are typically used for imbalances with this chakra are Mimulus, Agrimony and Cerato.

Rachael needed Mimulus to help her address some of her known fears. Mimulus can help her face her fears intellectually, rather than emotionally, so she can find ways of coping and moving forward in life. When Rachael starts communicating better, she may find that many of her fears can be conquered in new ways.

Agrimony will help Rachael because she masks her true feelings by role playing, joking, and distracting attention away from conflict. Behind the comical facade, though, she experiences real inner turmoil. Agrimony will help her communicate her true feelings and trust that her opinions have value.

One of the hallmarks of a good communicator is the ability to listen to one's inner voice. We gave Rachael a shot of Cerato so that she can trust herself. It will give her the confidence that she needs to express her opinions, regardless of what others may think.

The throat chakra resonates with the color blue. Wearing blue can help you find your voice, feel confident in your ability to communicate effectively and express yourself. Surround yourself with blue if you want to tap into your feelings and creativity. We look forward to seeing Rachael's blue scarf on Broadway.

Chapter Six

Violet caught her reflection in a store window while she searched for the address. She was horrified by the reflected image. Yikes! How had she left her spot behind the pharmacy counter looking like that? Probably because Violet avoided mirrors and reflections at all costs. She had never been happy with the way she looked, unless you counted those cute pictures of her when she was about six. Today, however, was particularly bad. Her hair seemed to be flying in all directions and she looked quite like the "dragon lady" the staff called her behind her back. Well, it hardly made sense to fix her hair when she was going to get a haircut.

She wondered if her front cashier, who had recommended this place, was sending her on a wild goose chase. Perhaps she wanted to get even because Violet had started to cut back on the girl's shifts. Violet had a bad feeling about the girl even before hiring her, but she looked really qualified on paper and had answered all the questions appropriately. And, she did have a great haircut, which was why, in a vulnerable moment, Violet had asked her where she had her hair done. The cashier had assured her that the salon was always happy to take walk-ins. So there she was, struggling to find the place. Violet rechecked her hand-drawn map, looked up at the street signs, and realized she should be seeing a hair salon. But, instead, she was looking at a bar.

"Well, doesn't that just make sense," Violet muttered. She suspected the cashier was a bit of a drinker, if not a recreational drug abuser. Forget the hair appointment. Violet pushed open the door, deciding to investigate. She would talk to the bartender. Perhaps the cashier was spending her breaks drinking in a bar. Then Violet would have grounds for terminating the girl's contract.

As soon as she opened the door, Violet was surrounded by the thick, heavy, sticky-smooth smell of caramel. She grabbed the hand rail of the steps for balance as she entered the bar. The smell was making her light-headed. It reminded her of the trips to the carnival she used to take as a kid: the smell of caramel apples and fudge, the mystery and intrigue. She remembered riding the carousel until the whole world spun around her and she was sick with dizziness.

Violet almost fell onto a bar stool and was grateful for the solid counter to hold on to while she planted her feet firmly on the floor. She took a deep breath to clear the overwhelming flashback from her mind.

"You'll be needing today's special."

Violet considered that neither the special nor the bartender matched her idea of what should be expected in a bar establishment. Rather than being some kind of deep-fried alcohol absorbent food or a bowl of salty nuts to encourage continuous thirst, the special appeared to be an incredible dessert. The top caramel layer of the concoction was obviously the source of the intoxicating smell.

"Go ahead! Indulge yourself," the bartender said as she passed Violet a spoon.

No wonder she was reminded of the carnival. With her

long, grey, braided hair, her worn jeans, and plaid flannel shirt, you could almost mistake her for someone's slightly eccentric grandmother. But the amethyst necklace, the turquoise wrist bangles, and the large silver hoop earrings fit in with the gypsy carnival theme decorations that populated all corners of the room. Violet wouldn't have been surprised to see a crystal ball appear on the bar. Yet, the bartender seemed quite down-to-earth in a way that couldn't be described. Violet was reminded of her own grandmother, who she figured would have pegged the bartender as an old soul or a wise woman.

Violet concentrated on the dainty purple glass bowl of dessert in order to distract herself from uncomfortable memories.

From the first bite, Violet was hooked. The cream mixture tasted a bit like yogurt and mixed with the grapes it was a healthy, wholesome combination. The smooth caramel added a layer of flavour that was almost sinful. Together, they were divine.

Violet raked at her hair with her free hand, making some pieces stick up while different ones fell down in front of her eyes.

"You're smart to let your hair grow," Violet said as she admired the Wise Woman's neat braids. "And to let it go grey is a smart move as well. I keep feeling like I'd like to do that, but it seems that a pharmacist shouldn't have hair in that growing-out stage where it gets into everything and looks so unkempt. Now, he's got great hair." Violet pointed her spoon at the black cat, who sat at the far end of the bar, keeping his distance. Still, Violet wondered what the food and restaurant licensing board would think of a cat being in the establishment. She scoured the dessert for signs of cat hair, and considered the fact that her hands were probably covered in bacteria. She tried to count calories in her head.

"I'll probably have to work out an extra fifteen minutes this week if I have any hope of keeping this caramel off my thighs," Violet calculated. "Not that it will make much of a difference. I look like a wreck, no matter what I do, or how much I exercise. I might as well enjoy the food, I'm so disgusting anyway." Violet noticed with disdain how her thighs spread across the bar stool like large jelly-rolls.

When she blew errant strands of hair out of her eyes, she could see there was a shot glass sitting beside her dessert. As much as she felt like having a shot of something — heck, anything — she couldn't possibly drink before six in the evening.

"I think I would be better off with just a glass of water," she said politely.

"This isn't alcohol." The Wise Woman pushed the shot glass closer to Violet. "This is a few drops of the Bach Flower essence Crab Apple."

Violet sat up straighter, let go of her hair, and lifted the shot glass to her nose. "Strange, I've been reading about Bach flower essences," she admitted. "I'm kind of curious about some of the natural lines of healing and have been researching a few. I guess from what I've read, it couldn't hurt to try."

"Crab Apple is considered the 'cleansing essence' from Dr. Bach's line," the Wise Woman said with a smile. "It won't make your hair grow any faster, or change your metabolism, but it might help you feel better about yourself in the meantime. It's indicated for people who feel an obsessive need to clean, are overly concerned with body odours, or unpleasant physical symptoms." Violet stole a glance at the cat, who was busy grooming himself. He stopped licking and twitched his tail at the Wise Woman. "Oh, Merlin," she muttered under her breath, as the cat jumped off the bar, and disappeared. "Crab Apple is also helpful for people who suffer from a poor self-image, or feel embarrassed by their physical appearance, or disgusted with their body."

"That sounds like something that could be very marketable," Violet said after she drained the shot glass. She twirled the glass absently, as though there might be answers hidden in the bottom. "You know, my employees complain that I'm too worried about cleanliness. They might be partially right. I think it's something I get from my mother." The Wise Woman smiled encouragingly and pulled up a stool to get comfortable. Merlin seemed to sense the opening as well and reappeared, settling in on the rafters.

"My mother was quite a dominant person when I was growing up and I think, in a way, she moulded me into the person I am today." Violet's right hand held the dessert spoon in a tight, but practiced grip. She waved the spoon in the air. "Even in this. As a young child, I favoured my left hand for things like eating, colouring, or writing. But my mother insisted that I use my right. Any time she saw me using my left, she would grab the utensil out of my hand and put it in my right. It didn't feel natural to me, but she said it was difficult to be left-handed in a right-handed world. I think she was afraid that I was too much like my grandmother. She was left-handed and proud of it." Violet switched the spoon to her left hand and words seemed to flow naturally as she continued with her story.

Violet explained that as a child, she often thought she saw and heard things that weren't really there. She used to spend a lot of time at her grandmother's, where her active imagination was encouraged. The bar seemed to disappear as Violet's mind retreated back to her grandmother's house. It had been filled with crystals, healing potions and plants, and the tinkling sound of wind chimes. It had been a peaceful place even though it always seemed filled with women. Violet recalled how she used to play in the parlour when people came to have Tarot cards or tea leaves read. She often helped while her grandmother made salves from beeswax and oils.

But when Violet was five, her grandmother suddenly died. Violet's mother seemed to erase every piece of Violet's grandmother after her death. She sold the house and burned, sold, or gave away all the personal effects that had been so much a part of her grandmother's life. After that, Violet's mother seemed different as well. She seemed afraid of anything that wasn't practical and scientific. She told Violet she was just "making stuff up" and "talking crazy" on the rare occasions when Violet tried to explain that she had "known" something was going to happen before it actually did.

When Violet expressed an interest in chemistry and biology, her parents bought her chemistry sets and a microscope. They encouraged her to find out why things happened the way they did. When Violet talked about wanting to make medicines, her mother warned her of the dangers of poisonous plants, and steered her towards becoming a "legitimate pharmacist."

Violet admitted that she didn't remember picking a university, or signing up for courses. It just seemed like something that happened to her with her mother's help. When Violet finished university, her mother had helped finance the purchase of a drug store franchise that Violet owned and operated. The store was very successful, and she put in long hours overseeing the pharmacy, as well as the over-the-counter lines.

Thinking about the business seemed to bring Violet back to the present. She switched the spoon over to her right hand and scooped up the last of the grapes from the dish. Merlin crept closer in case some of the last ones had jumped out of the bowl.

"Do you enjoy owning a business?" the Wise Woman asked, shifting a bit on her stool.

"Oh, it's very successful." Violet focused on the Wise Woman's earrings, while she considered the question further. "I seem to have a lot of problems with the employees, though. They don't like me; that's for sure. They call me the 'dragon lady'. They think I boss and bully them around. I know the best way to run the business. So they need to fall in line or I won't be bothered keeping them around. I hire people according to their credentials, and I order stock according to computer charts, formulas, and projections. My husband often wants to go by what feels right or by his gut feelings. But that's just hocus pocus. I run a tight ship, and I sign the cheques."

While Violet paused to scrape the last of the caramel from the bowl, the Wise Woman rose and poured another shot. She placed it in front of Violet and nodded at her to drink it.

"More Crab Apple?" asked Violet. "I'll have to research the dosage on these Bach Flowers."

"This one is Vine." The Wise Woman watched Violet drink it. "Vine will help you remain determined without dominating other people. It will help you encourage people, rather than control them. Sometimes we learn to control people because of how we were treated as a child. You might have learned that controlling others achieves a certain result. Vine might help you give up the fierce need to control, so you can pause and listen to your intuitive side."

"Hmm . . . " Violet set down the shot glass and lined it up precisely with the first one. "You know, when I first came into your bar, I smelled that caramel and I remembered being a kid at the carnival. I've always felt really drawn to gypsies, fortune telling, and the psychic stuff, but I purposely stay away from it. I think that I'm afraid it may open up a part of me that I'm not prepared to see."

The Wise Woman busied herself wiping down the bar. "Like your grandmother, maybe?"

Violet nodded slowly. "You know, I don't think I've ever admitted that until now, but yes, you're right. I think I am a bit like her. I'm fascinated by intuition and some of the healing things she did, and yet I'm terrified of it."

Violet barely noticed Merlin curl up on her lap. She stroked him absently while he purred. The Wise Woman smiled.

"I'm really drawn to branching into some of the more natural healing brands, like the Bach Flowers, for instance, and maybe homeopathic remedies. I'd like to study them more and sell them in the store. I feel that it might be a nice balance if I could offer scientific, conventional options, as well as some of the traditional lines. I've talked to my husband about it, and he is all for it. He says it 'feels right'. The numbers don't really support it, from a sales point of view. But you know what? I think I'd like to give it a try anyway." Violet paused for breath, and looked fondly at Merlin. The Wise Woman placed another shot glass at her place. Being careful not to disturb Merlin, she reached for the glass.

"This is Walnut. It will help you adapt to the change as

you start to incorporate your intuition into your scientific way of thinking. It is especially useful for anyone going through a major life change, and it sounds to me like you are going through one. Walnut is helpful when you are eager to move forward, but still feel a bit held back by a stronger personality, links with the past, or other circumstances."

Violet raised her shot glass. "Cheers to my mother!" She downed the shot. "I understand why she did the things she did, but I'm ready to move on and be my own person now."

She gently lifted Merlin from her lap and hugged him to her chest. She was about to set him down on the stool beside her when she realized something was there. It was a small paperback book wrapped in a purple headband. Setting Merlin on the counter, Violet held up the package for inspection. "What's this, and where did it come from?"

The Wise Woman shrugged and gestured to Merlin. "That Merlin, he always knows just what a person needs to take with them on the journey. Open it up—it's for you."

Violet uncoiled the headband and put it on, slicking her hair underneath it. Just as she wished she could see her reflection, the Wise Woman handed her a mirror. She was astonished to realize the headband fixed her hairdo. "Wow, this will work until the crazy parts grow out." Violet scratched behind Merlin's ear in thanks.

She glanced at the book title and read it aloud: *The Violet Flame*. She felt that strange dizzy sensation again. This time, it felt almost comforting. As she opened the cover, she found an inscription on the front page in familiar handwriting: "To My Violet—A Kindred Spirit. Enjoy your gifts, knowing you are always protected. Love you always, Grandma Willow."

The old Violet might have rejected the gift, but the new Violet felt a lump in her throat that prevented any further discussion. Instead, she smiled her appreciation at the Wise Woman, and bent to kiss Merlin, leaving a tear on his head. She raised her hand to wave from the doorway and stepped into a new life.

As she reached into her handbag for a tissue to wipe the tears, Violet realized she hadn't paid her bill. She turned around and discovered that a vacant lot had replaced the bar. Something purple caught her eye and she bent down to examine a small patch of grass. Growing out of the asphalt and dirt was a lone, wild violet—perfect in its presentation. Violet's first thought was to pick it and save it as evidence of her strange encounter. She could transplant it to a safer environment. Instead, she gently parted the grass around the flower, allowing it to bloom in all its glory in its chosen spot.

A Note from the Wise Woman

Violet visited us with issues pertaining to the third eye chakra. This sixth chakra is located above and between the eyebrows and is sometimes referred to as the brow chakra. The main issues of this chakra are intuition and wisdom. The goal of balanced development for this chakra is to be able to "see" with something other than with the eyes. It is about being able to connect feelings and a sense of higher knowing with thoughts. When this chakra is balanced, you are charismatic and highly intuitive. You are not attached to material things as much as you are focused on pursuing your inner purpose.

This chakra doesn't correspond to any particular age of development. For some people, it may be well-developed and balanced early on in life. For others, it may develop much later, perhaps due to a particular significant event. For a lot of people, like Violet, it may be well-developed in childhood but become blocked or unbalanced, returning as an issue to be dealt with in later years.

If this chakra spins too fast, or is too open, you may be highly logical, dogmatic, an authoritarian or arrogant. This was Violet's experience. The left side of her brain is very dominant. She's a perfectionist, and doesn't allow herself to accept failings in herself, or others.

A blocked third eye chakra can result in the fear of success. This may manifest as someone who is undisciplined. As they block their inner wisdom and fear their insights and feelings, these people sometimes force themselves to abide by a set of rules that becomes limiting and frightening. This can even result in mental illness.

I made caramel cream grapes for Violet. There aren't a lot of foods that resonate with the sixth chakra. As you move up with the chakras to higher realms, the material world including food has a lesser importance. Grapes do have a connection to the third eye chakra, partially because of their colour. We knew that the caramel would provide a special connection for Violet and the contrasts in this dessert help connect her practical and playful sides.

The Bach Flowers that are typically indicated for imbalances with this chakra are Crab Apple, Vine, and Walnut.

Because Violet's chakra is spinning so fast and blocking her intuition, she is trying desperately to control everything in her world. Her scientific logical thoughts don't match what she sees in the mirror, despite her efforts to mould and control. Crab Apple can help her accept her imperfections. As she balances her third eye, she will be more in touch with her body and be better able to work with rather than against it.

Violet's need for Vine developed from her upbringing. She was controlled by her mother and learned to emulate that controlling nature in her interactions with others. Any time Violet appeared to branch out and connect with her intuition, or a reality that her mother didn't understand, she was returned to the material, physical reality. Even her natural tendency to write with her left hand was "corrected." This may have contributed to a blocked chakra. Vine can help soften and gentle Violet's personality. She can be determined without having to dominate so she can follow her inner voice without the need to seek out scientific proof.

For Violet, Walnut will serve as a support as she balances her chakra. It isn't easy to undue past patterns of behaviour even when you know the path you walk is right for you. Walnut will help Violet let go of the past and continue to move through the changes, despite what her mother may say!

The colour purple resonates with the third eye chakra. Wearing purple around the brow area, like Violet's headband, can help you connect to your wisdom and subconscious insights. Violet's grandmother was right about *The Violet Flame*. The violet flame is believed by many to be a healing energy used for transformation and protection. This small book includes a poem that was grounding and helpful to Violet's grandmother, and had a meaningful connection to Violet, considering her name. Merlin thinks that by the time Violet's hair has grown to a decent style, she's going to be remarkably transformed.

Chapter Seven

Norma had given up trying to get a good sleep. She had tried warm milk, a good book, searching the Internet, and inputting work updates. Every time she tried to settle into sleep her mind kept on going, thinking about things she should have said to clients and ways she could have done things differently. She replayed the events of the day, the weeks, and the months.

Finally, she gave up, pulled on a pair of comfortable jeans, and an old sweatshirt of her husband's that she hadn't been able to part with. She grabbed her purse and car keys and took off for a drive. At the last moment she had put her new digital camera with a high powered lens in her purse. She didn't really expect to find any photography subjects out and about at four in the morning, but you never knew.

She drove aimlessly, without a clear destination. Norma let her mind wander to earlier times in her life, when she and her husband had taken the colicky twins for drives in the car to get them to sleep. She remembered Sunday drives for ice-cream in out-of-the-way places, and visits to farmer's markets. In later years she and Earl had driven to country bed and breakfasts on weekend getaways, enjoying the journey even more than the destination.

The tears pooled as she remembered the last drive she

had with Earl. In a reversal of roles, she had been the one behind the wheel, while he sat in the passenger seat. The cancer was in its final stages. They had driven until they reached a deserted beach. Earl wasn't strong enough to get out of the car, so Norma had driven onto the sand. They rolled down the windows and inhaled the salt spray while they talked. The gulls screamed while Norma and Earl cried together and discussed his inevitable death. Norma had agreed to carry on, to live her life and enjoy herself. At the time, with him beside her, she almost believed she could.

A mother and child had walked onto the beach while they were talking. Needing some air, Norma got out of the car and asked if she could take their pictures. The child had been full of life and vitality, and Norma captured that in a close up shot. It had, like many of Norma's portraits, captured the very essence of the child.

When Norma returned to the car she had a moment of panic, and thought Earl was dead. She hesitated before checking his pulse. His eyes had opened when she touched his neck, and for the first time Norma knew the real Earl was no longer there, even though his body hung on. Norma kept a copy of the child's picture on her bedside table. It reminded her there was a cycle to life and death. Because the tears were freely flowing now, Norma pulled over to the side of the road to collect herself. As she blew her nose and dried her cheeks she glanced around to see where she was. She had parked in front of a bar of some sort. Strangely, at just past four in the morning, the lights were glowing in a welcoming, soft, orange, and Norma could see movement through the lacy curtains. Someone was obviously in there moving around. The neon sign on the door flashed the word "Open" at her in a commanding way.

The Wise Woman was just putting a finishing crown of whipped cream on three individual Raspberry Angel Cloud servings when Norma pushed open the door.

Norma inhaled and braced herself for the inevitable smell of perfumes, soaps, and various cosmetics. She automatically reached in her purse for her package of allergy tablets, but stopped short in amazement. As she analysed the smell, something she was now quite good at considering the scent free condition of her home and office, she realized it smelled like nothing! That wasn't quite true—it smelled like bed sheets after they had been washed in borax, not treated with any chemicals, and allowed to dry on the line. It was a pure, fresh, outdoors smell. It was a smell that many cosmetics tried to reproduce, and in the process left Norma struggling to breathe as she scratched away rashes.

As Norma took in the immaculate surroundings she nodded her head in scent-free, chemical-free approval. The white lilies that adorned every table were obviously real, and a delight, even as they flooded her with bittersweet memories. Norma realized that she was alone in the establishment, with the exception of the bartender.

"You'll be needing the special." The bartender placed a small white china plate in front of Norma as she took a seat at the bar. The plate seemed too fragile to even support the red and white dessert that was so artfully displayed. The red seemed a startling contrast to the whipped cream topping. Norma considered that the bartender looked nothing like what one would expect. But then she wasn't sure what one did expect in a bar that appeared to be decorated more like something out of Better Homes and Gardens, that was in the middle of nowhere and open at four in the morning. The bartender looked like a weathered gardener in her purple flannel shirt and neatly braided grey hair. Norma almost expected to see grass and dirt stains on the knees of her worn jeans, but they were as clean as everything else in the place. Norma decided that she would have labelled a close-up portrait of the bartender "Wise Woman".

Norma was startled from her observation by an indignant meow. She had almost placed her purse on a cat lying on the stool beside her. He appeared so lifeless Norma hadn't even noticed him. Although he yowled at her and blinked his eyes, he showed no intention of moving. He yawned as she carefully switched her purse to the opposite stool.

Norma usually controlled her diet quite strictly, in part because of her chemical sensitivities, which seemed to extend to food as well as scents, but she realized she had been driving around all night and needed sustenance. The last thing she had was a mug of warm milk, and that had been a long time ago.

"I was going to say I better not, as this will keep me up all night, but it looks like it's a bit late for that," Norma said as she glanced at her watch and realized it was almost morning. "I guess I could call this breakfast." Norma picked up a dessert fork, admiring its precisely correct position to the left of the plate.

She controlled a surprisingly childish urge to dig into the jell-o flavoured raspberries, whipped cream, and spongy cake. Instead, she gently sliced off a small piece with her fork. She was careful to not press hard on the delicate plate. As soon as it reached her taste buds Norma remembered lying on a picnic blanket in a grassy field, staring up at puffy white clouds.

"We used to lay on our backs with the kids and have contests imagining shapes in the clouds. Often all five of us would fall asleep for a few minutes in the warm sunshine." Norma didn't stop to consider that the bartender would have no idea what she was talking about. The thought just seemed to come clear out of the blue, and yet the Wise Woman smiled in complete understanding.

"If only I could sleep so well now." Norma glanced at her watch again. "I don't think I've had a good night's sleep since before the kids started school and I started working. And that's a lifetime ago." Norma considered that the Wise Woman was probably used to hearing tales of not sleeping, considering the hours this bar was open, so she decided to describe her lack of slumber in detail. Norma explained how she would gratefully crawl in bed every night, bone tired from the events of the day, but as soon as her head hit the pillow the record player that was her mind turned on. Lying there in the dark, she would replay every conversation she had with clients. She would reconsider the approach she had taken with them. If she had rephrased things would they have invested wiser, listened to her financial acuity, and set up their financial lives better? Investment numbers spun around in her head.

Norma explained to the Wise Woman that she didn't worry about the financial advice she gave people. She was very confident in her abilities; she had built a strong company from nothing and had tremendous financial success herself. Her children were all well taken care of through their old age due to her investments. It wasn't exactly worry that kept her awake; it was more like a frustration with those that didn't heed her advice. She kept thinking that there was a way she could pound it into young people's minds that you make your own luck; you don't get anything handed to you in life. The mental arguments would just go around and around in a never-ending looped recording.

Norma raised her head from her dessert to see if the Wise Woman was even listening, and realized a shot glass had appeared beside her plate.

"Oh, I don't think alcohol will help the problem, and anyway, I'm driving." Norma pulled the car keys from her jean pocket and placed them on the bar for emphasis.

"It's not alcohol. It's a shot of the Bach Flower essence White Chestnut." The Wise Woman wiped the already spotless bar as she explained. "White Chestnut is often helpful for people that can't sleep due to mental restlessness. White Chestnut can break the mental pattern of the recording. Worry and frustration can be replaced with trust in a positive outcome. That peace of mind can bring relief in the form of a good night's sleep." Wise Woman gestured towards Merlin, who was fast asleep on the bar stool.

"Well, I certainly could use some peaceful sleep, that's for sure. Heaven knows I'm not getting any peace at any other time." The thought of sleeping in peace brought tears to Norma's eyes. The shot glass' contents felt soothing as it slid past the gathering lump in her throat.

"Most times I think sleepless nights are just part of the package with me. I feel too old and tired to really bother trying to change anything now. Earl and I had all these plans, but now that he's gone, there just doesn't seem to be any point to it all."

At the mention of Earl's name, the Wise Woman pulled up a bar stool and sat directly across from Norma. She leaned her elbows on the table and settled in for a good listen. Refreshed from his nap, Merlin sat up, jumped on to the bar top, and took up position beside the Wise Woman.

Seeing as she had such an attentive audience, Norma carried on with her story.

"I never really wanted to be a financial consultant. It was just something that had to be done." Norma explained that Earl had been very good at providing for their family, as he had risen to upper management throughout his career, but he had no idea how to save, invest, or spend wisely. Norma had been the one that managed the family finances. She read all the books and went to investment training seminars. When friends started finding out she knew a lot about finances they came to her for free advice, and in time Norma started up her own financial consulting business.

"I wanted to pay off the house and the cars, have university education tucked away for the kids, and have us be secure enough that I could follow my passion for photography." Norma twirled her fork through the last of the whipped cream and smiled. She explained how somewhere along the way they got used to the money, the benefits, and the lifestyle. Quitting hadn't seemed like an option after that. Two years ago she started developing chemical sensitivities, and had to eliminate all scents from the house and the office. She had to totally dismantle her dark room because of its chemicals. It seemed foolish to leave work and the group health benefits it provided.

"Then, clear out of the blue, less than a year before both of us were planning to retire, Earl got sick with cancer. He went from healthy and vibrant, still putting in fourteen hour days at work, to home in bed with an oxygen tank, and then palliative care, in what seemed like the blink of an eye. I always told him those cigarettes were going to kill him, but he had quit for me, because of my allergies. We thought the cough was just a side effect of the withdrawal, but it was the first sign of the lung cancer that had invaded him."

The Wise Woman reached for the Kleenex box underneath the bar and slid it over to Norma, who took one and twisted it around her fingers without stopping her story. She had taken a leave of absence to be with Earl, and nursed him through his final days. The office had run fine without her, and she had considered not going back after Earl died. But all her retirement plans and dreams didn't make sense anymore. They had planned to travel together; he would golf and she would look for characters to photograph.

"I go to the office every day because I don't know what else to do. I don't have the energy to do anything else." Norma looked directly into the Wise Woman's eyes. "To be honest, I'm jealous of Earl. He got to leave. I know he's in a peaceful place, and I'm left here with tons of possessions and supposed comforts, but they're objects that mean nothing and bring me no peace."

Norma seemed to finally notice the twisted tissue in her hand, and wiped the tears briskly from her cheeks and blew her nose. As she scanned the room for a garbage can, she noticed another shot glass had been placed before the first. Not even caring what was in it, she raised it to lips that felt hot and parched from talking and crying. She drank the cool liquid in one swallow.

"That's the Bach Flower essence Wild Rose." The Wise Woman's voice almost seemed a whisper in the stillness of the bar. Norma leaned in to catch every word.

"Wild Rose will help you find the energy you need to improve things and move on with your life. Rather than rely on support from others, Wild Rose will help you find the support you need to change your life circumstances from within. It can help motivate you."

"That is exactly what I need." For the first time since she walked into the bar, Norma seemed to come alive. Merlin jumped from the bar to the stool beside her and batted at her leg with his front paw, as though testing the solidity of her lap. She moved her arm to make way for him and lightly patted her leg.

"Come on over, I could use the company."

Norma patted Merlin absently while he settled in. "I really do want to come out of this heavy sadness. I know it's time. And it's not just about Earl's death. It's about something inside me that really wants to come out. It feels like it has been squished inside for a long time. I'm not really sure what it is, but it feels like a solidness that needs to become lighter, and free itself."

While Merlin purred, Norma tried to explain how she felt that she could really make a difference in the world, but the financial world of material gain seemed so unimportant and insignificant. She didn't want to follow stock trends anymore, or look at new investment portfolios. She wanted to connect with people and help them connect to the soul within. That inside essence of people seemed so obvious when she captured a still moment from a fast moving world with the click of her camera.

The Wise Woman nodded, and placed a third shot glass in front of Norma. As Norma drank, the Wise Woman explained the contents.

"That is the Bach Flower essence Star of Bethlehem. Star of Bethlehem is often helpful when you've suffered a shock or trauma, such as the death of a loved one. It's called the comforter and soother of pain and sorrow. But it's a lot more than that. Merlin calls it the butterfly essence, because it helps with transformation. It's painful for a butterfly to come out of the heaviness and safety of its cocoon, but the wonderful feeling of spreading new wings and flying is worth the effort. Star of Bethlehem can help you during the process."

Norma and the Wise Woman both stared at Merlin. Norma seemed to see him in a new light. The Wise Woman smiled knowingly.

"He's a lot more than just a cat, isn't he?" The Wise Woman nodded in agreement as Norma gently placed him back on the stool beside her. The sun was just starting to peak over the horizon, and Merlin went off to investigate in the morning light as Norma gathered her things.

Norma picked up her car keys and noticed that where the Kleenex box had been there sat a gigantic white hat. She hadn't seen the Wise Woman set it on the bar, but she must have.

"Are you going out to garden?" Norma asked the Wise Woman, gesturing towards the hat.

"Oh, that's not mine, that's for you — a gift from Merlin." The Wise Woman handed the hat over to Norma.

She considered how large, wild, and eclectic the hat was. It seemed to be woven of some kind of hemp material, but it was as white as the whipped cream on her dessert — it was almost blinding in its whiteness. Wrapped over the crown of the hat was a gauze-like scarf that poked through holes on either side of the hat, and extended as long tails that Norma assumed were to be tied under the chin to secure the hat in place. The gauze scarf was as colourful as the hat was white. It was covered in bright butterflies; coloured brilliantly in combinations of red, orange, yellow, green, blue, and purple. The scarf was so light that when it moved the butterflies seemed to flutter and dance.

Norma hesitated for a moment before placing the hat on her head. It fit perfectly. She realized the brim was just right for keeping the sun from her eyes while she peered through her camera lens.

She met the Wise Woman's eyes as she stood by the door of the bar. No words were exchanged, but the message was clear.

Norma stepped into the morning sunshine. She inserted the key in the ignition and started the car. She pressed the rarely used button that folded down the top of the convertible. While she waited for it to fully open, she tied the butterflies under her chin. Norma resisted the urge to look back in her rear view mirror. No more looking back for her. "I'll bring the past forward with me," Norma said, to no one but herself. She drove toward the sunrise.

A Note from the Wise Woman

Norma came to Merlin and me in the middle of the night with issues of the seventh or crown chakra. This chakra, the highest of the primary chakras, is located at the top, or crown, of your head. This chakra is considered your connection to a greater consciousness, or the divine self. Development of spirituality and selflessness are its primary goals. When this chakra is balanced, people are often said to be magnetic in their personality. Others are drawn to them. There is a peace that comes with this clear connection to spirit and awareness. You realize that all things are possible.

Like the sixth chakra, seventh chakra development doesn't often correspond with a particular age. A well functioning seventh chakra is likely developed as a result of a multitude of events that can occur at any age, or stage, in life. For many people, as is the case for Norma, a shocking event such as trauma or death of a loved one may be the catalyst that encourages you to take a look at this connection.

If this chakra spins too fast you may feel apathetic or depressed, exhibit a sense of frustration at your unrealized potential, or find yourself lacking focus.

Similarly, a blocked crown chakra may create a sense of exhaustion. Decisions become difficult. People with blocked crown chakras may feel they have lost their reason for being.

People with unbalanced crown chakras often become quite egocentric and focused on material possessions. In order to maintain the illusion of control over the material world, they develop into workaholics or become quite mechanical in their actions. A traumatic event often leaves them floundering as they lose control, and they begin longing for the true meaning of life.

There aren't a lot of foods that resonate with the crown chakra, but Merlin is a big believer in feeding all our guests, so we make Raspberry Angel Clouds for crown chakra issues. Merlin thinks the angel food is very appropriate, as it symbolizes the connection with the spirit world. Both the cake and the whipped cream remind us of puffy, white, heavenly clouds. The deep red of the raspberries encourages the need to bring a spiritual connection deep into your physical core to your most basic root chakra.

The Bach Flowers that are often helpful for imbalances with this chakra are White Chestnut, Wild Rose, and Star of Bethlehem.

White Chestnut is very helpful for anyone that can't sleep because they can't shut off their mind. It may be particularly helpful for people that are moving mechanically through the day, getting by on routine and established patterns. When the mechanical actions of the day are stopped the mind often continues on with mental arguments and cyclical conversations. White Chestnut can help break that pattern of internal conversation.

Wild Rose matches Norma's (and Merlin's) sense of apathy or lack of motivation. Norma's lack of motivation has developed into her approach to life. This sense of resignation or surrender often comes from a traumatic event or change in circumstances that leaves people feeling they have lost control. Norma may have been relying on Earl for support, instead of finding her strength from within. Wild Rose will help her accept responsibility for her life and circumstances. Once she has gained this acceptance, she can focus on her true passion and find the meaning that is lacking in her life.

Norma has been shocked into a transformation. This is common for people that are developing their crown chakra. People need Star of Bethlehem to support the pain or discomfort that often accompanies such growth. Merlin is very wise to see Star of Bethlehem as the butterfly essence; as Norma sheds her cocoon and gains her wings of freedom, she will find Star of Bethlehem a great comfort.

The Crown Chakra resonates with the colour white. White is considered the ultimate luminescence, and is the colour of purity and spirit. Norma liked our white lilies because they helped her feel clean, pure, and renewed. The white lotus flower is used as a symbol for the crown chakra. Surrounding yourself with white can provide a very peaceful connection—wearing a white hat, for instance, can provide such a connection. The butterfly scarf is Merlin's personal touch, and knowing the way Norma drives, he figures she'll need it to keep her hat on!

Let Merlin and Wise Woman teach you to make the foods they used to help Samantha, Lola, Simone, Jeanne, Rachael, Violet, and Norma, and be a Wise Woman right in your own kitchen!

Chapter One
Ginger Cookies

Merlin tried to be patient while he watched Wise Woman from his perch on the kitchen window sill. His soft black ears twitched ever so slightly as if listening to ghost whispers. His intense yellow eyes never left the Wise Woman as she gathered the familiar ingredients.

"Sorry, Merlin, here comes the mixer."

Merlin twitched his sleek tail in irritation at the noise. He watched the Wise Woman, knowing she was consulting a cookbook in her head and a knowing in her heart as she added ingredients to the bright red glazed bowl.

2 ¼ (550 ml) cups all purpose flour
1 tsp (5ml) Baking soda
¼ tsp (1.25 ml) cloves
½ tsp (2.5 ml) cinnamon
1tsp (5 ml) ground ginger
¼ tsp (1.25 ml) salt
¾ cup (175 ml) butter
1 cup (250 ml) brown sugar
1 egg
¼ cup (50 ml) molasses
1 tsp (5 ml) minced ginger
½ tsp (2.5 ml) lemon zest
¾ cup (175ml) chocolate chips or chocolate chunks (optional)

Directions:
1. Preheat the oven to 350° F
2. Whisk the butter and brown sugar in a bowl until it is light and fluffy.
3. Add egg, molasses, fresh ginger and lemon zest to the mixture.
4. Gradually add the flour and the remaining dry ingredients until the dough is combined.
5. (Optional) Add chocolate chips or chunks.
6. Let the mixture set in the fridge for several minutes, until firm enough to roll.
7. Use a tablespoon to create little balls of cookie dough, and place them on a parchment-lined baking sheet, about 2 inches apart from eachother.
8. Gently squish the center of each dough ball with a fork to create ridges.
9. Place cookies in the oven for 10 minutes.

Chapter Two
Vanilla Cardamom Pudding

Merlin couldn't help himself. There is something about seeing a container of cream that makes a cat lick his nose in anticipation. Merlin managed to divert the reflex into an excuse to wash his face and whiskers but as he bowed his face he continued to peer through his paw as Wise Woman poured the thick white liquid into a heavy bottomed saucepan.

Wise Woman didn't look up from her work by the stove but said, "Don't you worry. You know I'll give you some. Merlin."

2 cups (500 ml) cream or whole milk
4 whole green cardamom pods
½ a vanilla bean (or 1 tbsp. (15 ml) Vanilla extract)
1/3 cup (75 ml) packed brown sugar

3 tbsp.(45ml) Corn starch
Pinch of salt

Directions:
1. Pour 2 cups of cream or whole milk into a heavy-bottomed saucepan, and heat on medium-low.
2. Crack the cardamom pods and drop the beans into the milk.
3. Add vanilla extract, and stir continuously.
4. Once small bubbles have begun to form at the edge of the pan, turn off the heat, cover, and let the spices steep in the milk for approximately 10 minutes.
5. Pour the flavoured milk mixture through a strainer and into a small mixing bowl.
6. Add brown sugar, cornstarch and salt to the now empty saucepan, and then whisk in the flavoured milk.
7. Reheat the saucepan on medium-low.
8. Mix until the pudding has reached the desired consistency.
9. Place pudding in bowls and set in refrigerator, and let cool for 2-3 hours.

Chapter Three
Pavlova

Merlin couldn't get Wise Woman's attention. He kept slinking back and forth between the kitchen and the bar meowing and rubbing up against her legs. He tried chasing Wise Woman's dusting cloth as she polished the bar top, but she just kept humming and polishing, so he tried sitting down on the cloth instead. That got her playing with him. It was rather fun, but it also made him dizzy, wasn't very dignified, and it really wasn't the attention he was looking for. He wanted her to go into the kitchen and do something with those eggs in the bright yellow bowl. Merlin didn't figure they were doing anybody any good just sitting there in the bowl. *With all the steps and waiting involved in this recipe, Merlin knew if she didn't get started, they would be up all night and Merlin had better things to do during a full moon night than make pavlova.*

6 egg whites (reserve 2 yolks for the filling)
¼ tsp. (1.25 ml) Salt
1 ½ tsp. (7.5ml) Cream of tarter
1 ½ cups (375ml) white sugar
1 tsp.(5ml) Vanilla
1 lemon pie filling
½ cup (125ml) Whipping cream (optional)
1 tbsp. (15ml) lemon zest (optional for topping)
Select fruits (optional)

Directions:
1. Preheat oven to 250° F
2. Crack 6 eggs and filter the whites into a bowl by transferring the egg yolks back and forth between the two half-shells of each egg. Place 2 of the yolks in a separate bowl and set them aside.
3. Beat egg whites, adding salt and cream of tartar, until stiff but not dry.
4. Add white sugar, 2 tablespoons at a time, mixing continuously.
5. Add vanilla while mixing, again until stiff.
6. Place large dollops of the meringue base around the inside of a heavy white casserole baking dish, leaving space in the middle.
7. Cover the dish with a sheet of parchment paper and place in the oven.
8. Bake for 2 hours.
9. After 2 hours, turn off the oven and let the pavlova sit in the oven for several hours to dry out.

10. Boil water in a double boiler, and mix the 2 egg yolks and lemon pie filling mix in the top, stirring until thickened.

11. Pour the lemon filling into the meringue base, filling up the hole in the middle, and covering everything but the tallest peaks of meringue.

12. Place in the fridge to cool.

13. Before serving, whip cream and add lemon zest. Top the casserole dish and decorate with fruits of your choosing.

Chapter Four
Molten Chocolate Cakes

Wise Woman removed the cakes from the oven. Merlin paced in between her legs and circled under the table while she traced a knife around the edge of each custard cup. He couldn't watch while she placed a plate on top of each cup and flipped the whole thing over so that the cake was inverted onto the plate. Merlin always worried that the cake would stick to the bottom of the custard cup.

"Don't worry, Merlin, they are all out okay."

4 ounces (4: 28gram squares) dark 70% cacao chocolate
2 ounces (2: 28 gram squares) unsweetened chocolate
½ cup (125ml) butter
3 eggs
1/3 cup (75 ml) white sugar
1 tsp. (5ml) vanilla extract
1/8 tsp. (1ml) cream of tarter
1 tbsp. (15 ml) white sugar
¼ cup (50 ml) icing sugar (optional)
Vanilla ice- cream (optional)

Directions:
1. Preheat oven to 400° F.

2. Melt the 6 squares of baking chocolate and butter using a double boiler. Stir occasionally.

3. Remove the top boiler pot from heat and set it aside.

4. Crack and separate the 3 egg whites, placing the egg whites into one bowl and the egg yolks in another.

5. Add 1/3 cup of sugar to the egg yolks, add vanilla, and beat until thick, pale, and fluffy.

6. Fold the melted chocolate mixture into the egg yolk mixture.

7. Add cream of tartar to the bowl of egg whites, rinse your egg beaters, and beat till the mixture makes peaks, adding a tablespoon of white sugar to the whites while beating.

8. Fold the stiff egg white mixture into the chocolate and egg yolk bowl.

9. Divide the batter into four buttered custard cups, filling each about 3/4.

10. Place cups on a cookie sheet and place in the oven for 10 minutes.

11. Remove from oven, and place a plate on top of each cup, flipping the cup and plate over so that the cake is inverted on the plate.

12. Add icing sugar as desired and serve with ice cream (optional).

Chapter Five
Peppermint Cheesecake

Merlin's throat was raw. It was burning and tickling at the same time. He kept trying to tell Wise Woman that there were no candy canes left over from Christmas. Considering that it was now September, that was hardly surprising. But every time he opened his mouth to meow, nothing came out.

"Okay, Merlin, I know what you're trying to say. Rest your voice, I'll use chocolate mints instead."

1 cup (250ml) chocolate graham crumbs
3 tbsp. (45ml) melted butter
3: 8 ounce (250ml) packages cream cheese
¾ cup (175ml) white sugar
3 eggs
1tsp. (5ml) Vanilla
¾ cup (175 grams or about 40 candies) crushed chocolate mint candies (or crushed candy canes)

Directions:
1. Preheat oven to 350 F.
2. Combine chocolate graham crumbs and butter.
3. Press the mixture into a buttered springform pan.
4. Place the crust in the oven for 10 minutes.
5. Unwrap and place the chocolate mint candies in a plastic bag, then crush the candies to pieces with a meat tenderizer.
6. Remove the crust from the oven and set it aside on a cooling rack.
7. Turn oven down to 325 F.
8. Place the 3 packages of cream cheese in a mixing bowl, and add sugar and a teaspoon of vanilla. Beat continuously while adding room-temperature eggs.
9. Add 1/2 cup of crushed candy and stir, then pour the mixture on top of the cooled crust.
10. Sprinkle the last 1/4 cup of candies on top of the batter.
11. Bake for 45 minutes.

Chapter Six
Carmel Cream Grapes

Merlin intended to stay in his typically relaxed position on the window sill. He supervised while the Wise Woman got things ready. He kept a close eye on her while she mixed ingredients in her purple mixing bowl. But, when a grape flew out of the bowl, bounced twice on the counter, three times on the floor, and rolled towards the table legs, Merlin was a goner. There is something about a rolling, bouncing, grape that connects all cats with their inner kitten. Maybe it's because most cats consider grapes more a toy than a true food item!

5 cups (1250ml) seedless red grapes
2 cups (500ml) sour cream
½ cup (125ml) sugar
2 tbsp. (30ml) vanilla
½ cup (125 ml) butter
½ cup (125 ml) brown sugar

Directions:
1. Wash and rinse grapes and remove any pieces of stem.
2. Mix sour cream, sugar, and vanilla in a bowl.
3. Add the grapes to the bowl and pour the mixture into a 9' x 13' pan.
4. Combine brown sugar and butter in a small saucepan over medium heat, stirring and bringing to a boil.
5. Remove from heat and pour the caramel evenly over the grape mixture without stirring.
6. Place the pan in the fridge and let cool.

<u>Chapter Seven</u>
Raspberry Angel Clouds

From his position on the window sill, Merlin felt the coolness of the evening air coming through the window and settling on his back. He watched as Wise Woman tore apart the angel food cake and placed pieces of it in a pan. He twitched his tail a bit as he watched her tear such irregular shapes. Some might have been one inch, others almost two. There was no rhyme or reason to her tearing, or to her placement of them in the pan. Merlin would have been much more uniform in his approach, but he did like the way the pieces of cake settled into the pan, looking like puffy clouds. As the supervisor, his job was only to intervene if the results were at stake. Merlin had tasted Wise Woman's Raspberry Angel Clouds enough to know the results would be perfect, even if never quite the same.

1 Angel food cake (Wise Woman uses the already-made version but you can start from scratch if you want)
1 pkg (170 g) raspberry-flavoured gelatin (8 serving size)
2 cups (500ml) raspberries (fresh or frozen)
2 cups (500ml) boiling water
½ cup (125ml) cold water
1 cup (250ml) whipping cream (optional)

Directions:
1. Tear apart and place angel food cake in a shallow 9' x 13' baking pan.
2. Fill a kettle with cold water and bring to a boil.
3. Empty raspberry jelly powder into a large bowl and mix with 2 cups boiling water, stirring until all the powder is dissolved.
4. Add two cups of fresh or frozen berries to the jelly mixture and stir, adding ½ cup of cold water to the mixture while stirring.
5. Pour the raspberry mixture on top of the angel food cake pieces, squishing down any pieces that puff up so that everything is covered.
6. Place in the refrigerator to cool and set.
7. Serve with whipped cream (optional).

Chakra Quick

Chakra	Main Focus	Age of Development
1- Root	Safety/Security; self reliance	1-8 years
2-Sacral	Independence; realize internal motivations	8-14 years
3-Solar	Sense of self; will-power; personal power	15-21 years
4-Heart	Love; relationships; acceptance of self	21-28 years
5-Throat	Communication; Self expression	28-35 years
6-Third Eye/Brow	Intuition and wisdom; Integration of Left and Right Brain	none
7- Crown	Connection to spirituality; selflessness	none

Reference Chart

Emotional Symptoms of Imbalance

Fear; emotionally needy; unfocused (escape the present)

Addictions; uncontrolled drives; mental exhaustion; compulsiveness; guilt;

Self-pity; jealous; aggression; judgemental; workaholic; insecure

Possessive love; unclear boundaries; fear of rejection;

Arrogant; over-talkative; afraid to express self; nervous; hides true feelings

Authoritarian; Highly logical; undisciplined; mental illness

Apathy; depressed; exhaustion; difficulty making decisions; egocentric

Chakra Quick

Chakra	Physical Symptoms of Imbalance
1- Root	Structural complaints (back pain; bone disease)
2-Sacral	Reproduction disorders; kidney disease; exhaustion
3-Solar	Sleep disorders; digestive complaints
4-Heart	Blood pressure problems; heart or lung disease
5-Throat	Sore throats; laryngitis; sore neck;
6-Third Eye/Brow	Headaches; sinusitis
7- Crown	Chronic exhaustion; sensitivities to pollution

Reference Chart

Corresponding Recipe	Bach Flowers	Color
Ginger Cookies	Rock Rose Sweet Chestnut Clematis	Red
Vanilla Cardamom Pudding	Oak Olive Pine	Orange
Pavlova	Impatiens Scleranthus Hornbeam	Yellow
Molten Chocolate Cakes	Red Chestnut Willow Chicory	Green
Peppermint Cheesecake	Mimulus Agrimony Cerato	Blue
Caramel Cream Grapes	Crab Apple Vine Walnut	Purple
Raspberry Angel Clouds	White Chestnut Wild Rose Star of Bethlehem	White

Heather MacKenzie-Carey is a Bach Flower Registered Practitioner living on the South Shore of Nova Scotia with her husband, daughter, a number of four legged creatures and perhaps a spirit or two.

Sweet Shack & Bach Bar is a reflection of Heather's personal shift from hard core medical science non-fiction, to the more flexible, sometimes magical, realms of vibrational energy healing, masked in fiction.

Heather tracks her journey with essence healing, Bach Flowers, homeopathic remedies, insightful books, moon phases, Chakras, and natural healing on her blog at www.PixieDustHealing.blogspot.com. Heather also shares her knowledge of Bach Flowers through private consultations for people and pets.

Heather is the author of Melvin's Balloons, a children's picture book that celebrates colors and their link to chakras and emotions, also available through Bryler Publications.

For more information visit Heather's website at www.PixieDustHealing.com.

Acknowledgements

As always, thanks and love to Tyla and Rick. Tyla, you are wise far beyond your years and in ways many can't even grasp. You are evidence of the evolutionary process of wise souls. I learn from you every day. Rick, you have been a constant throughout much of my personal chakra development, always balance my heart, encourage me to dream outside the box, follow my intuition, and are 50% responsible for Tyla! Both of you guys have also provided yourselves as willing Bach Flower essence subjects and food tasters! Our triangle feels very complete.

This manuscript would still be in the filing cabinet if it were not for Cynthia, Kathleen, and everyone at Bryler Publications. Thanks for your patience when I didn't have any! You do so much more work than most readers ever realize or appreciate. Thanks.

Finally, a special thanks to Sibylle who during the creation of this book took me on some pretty frequent trips to other dimensions, brought me back to earth, and inserted some commas here and there as well!

Thank you!

15% Off Bach Flower Consultation and Personalized Remedy

Want to see which Bach Flower Essences are indicated for you? Want to receive your own "Wise Woman write – up" and have a combination remedy bottle shipped to you?

Redeem this coupon and receive 15% off a personalized Bach Flower essence consultation with the author of Sweet Shack & Bach Bar.

For more information on the consultation process, visit Heather's website at www.pixiedusthealing.com. To redeem your coupon and book a consultation, email Heather at heather@pixiedusthealing.com